On The Road with Mr. Toad
Series Editor: Mark I. West

1. *A Children's Literature Tour of Great Britain*
   Mark I. West

A Children's Literature Tour of Great Britain

Mark I. West

On the Road with Mr. Toad, no. 1

The Scarecrow Press, Inc.
Lanham, Maryland • Toronto • Oxford
2003

SCARECROW PRESS, INC.

Published in the United States of America
by Scarecrow Press, Inc.
A wholly owned subsidiary of
The Rowman & Littlefield Publishing Group, Inc.
4501 Forbes Boulevard, Suite 200, Lanham, Maryland 20706
www.scarecrowpress.com

PO Box 317, Oxford, OX2 9RU, UK

Copyright © 2003 by Mark I. West

All rights reserved. No part of this publication may be reproduced, stored in a retrieval system, or transmitted in any form or by any means, electronic, mechanical, photocopying, recording, or otherwise, without the prior permission of the publisher.

British Library Cataloguing in Publication Information Available

Library of Congress Cataloging-in-Publication Data

West, Mark I.
   A children's literature tour of Great Britain / Mark I. West.
     p. cm. — (On the road with Mr. Toad; no. 1)
   Includes bibliographical references and index.
   ISBN 0-8108-4878-3 (pbk. : alk. paper)
   1. Children's literature, English—History and criticism. 2. Authors, English—Homes and haunts—Great Britain. 3. Literary landmarks—Great Britain. 4. Great Britain—In Literature. 5. Setting (Literature). I. Title. II. Series.
PR109.W47 2003
820.9'9282'0941—dc22
                                                                             2003015229

Manufactured in the United States of America.

○™ The paper used in this publication meets the minimum requirements of American National Standard for Information Sciences—Permanence of Paper for Printed Library Materials, ANSI/NISO Z39.48-1992.

For Nancy and Gavin, my fellow travelers

Contents

Foreword by Peter Hunt		ix
Acknowledgments		xi
Introduction		1
1	King Arthur	3
2	The Rev. W. Awdry and Christopher Awdry	11
3	Sir James M. Barrie	15
4	Michael Bond	19
5	Frances Hodgson Burnett	23
6	Lewis Carroll	27
7	John Cunliffe	35
8	Roald Dahl	39
9	Ian Fleming	43
10	Kenneth Grahame	47
11	Thomas Hughes	53

12	Charles Kingsley	59
13	Rudyard Kipling	63
14	Edward Lear	69
15	C. S. Lewis	75
16	A. A. Milne	79
17	E. Nesbit	85
18	Philippa Pearce	89
19	Beatrix Potter	93
20	Arthur Ransome	105
21	Robin Hood	109
22	Robert Louis Stevenson	113
23	J. R. R. Tolkien	117
24	Mary Tourtel	121
Selected Bibliography		125
Index		127
About the Author		133

Foreword

In Britain we have so much history that we are very careless about it. Within a two-mile radius of my (350-year-old) cottage in the Cotswold Hills are two Iron Age fortifications, a prehistoric long-barrow burial site, a still-inhabited fourteenth-century manor house, one of the largest and best-preserved Roman mosaics in Europe, and an uncompleted Victorian mansion. I have to confess, however, that the only time I visit them is when my American friends come to call. And we are equally careless about our literary heritage. We have had some of the greatest writers and illustrators for children in the world, but if you want to see their manuscripts or original artwork, you would do well to tour the great university libraries of North America (but that's another book!). Even Winnie-the-Pooh and his friends live in the New York Public Library.

If we have gotten rid of a great deal of paper, we can't get rid of the places, and these are what Mark's book is about—experiencing places. This is very important for readers, because the experience of stories does not stop at the covers of books. If you love children's books—and a great many people love children's books in a way that they do not love adults' books—then to breathe the air that the authors breathed, or to see the countryside or the houses that they transformed into fiction, is an extension of that love. Perhaps this is especially true when that countryside and those houses are not in your own country. My four daughters read Laura Ingalls Wilder's books to destruction, and so it was a curious pleasure for me to visit the house in Mansfield, Missouri, and look at Pa's violin. Similarly, having read *Make Way for Ducklings* to our girls when they were young, we enjoyed taking them to play on the duckling statues in the park in Boston.

This multidimensional experience is what fiction means: fiction and real life do not simply blur; fiction *becomes* real life—and if it didn't, fiction would not have the effect on us that it does. Thus, it is not romantic or whimsical to visit Paddington Station and find yourself half-looking for a small bear with a suitcase, or to look across Coniston Water in the Lake District and be slightly surprised that you *don't* see the small dinghies of the Swallows and the Amazons. Equally, although some of the sites that Mark lists in this book have undoubtedly been commercialized, to visit them is not to succumb to commercialism but to join a community of enthusiasts.

There is, then, a great deal to enjoy here—and some wonderful oddities. Why, one wonders, is there a *Wind in the Willows* experience in Derby, a city about as far from the idyllic Thames of the book as can be imagined, and when Kenneth Grahame, as far as known, never went there? Or why is Beatrix Potter so celebrated in Gloucester, simply because she set just one of her books there?

Armed with the Web sites and the detailed information that Mark has collected, readers are well equipped for a series of rich experiences. But I would like to add one more dimension to Mark's book: the landscapes. Britain is probably unique in the world in having such a large variety of landscapes in such a small space. In an easy day's drive, you can go from the harsh moorland of the Pennines to the gentle hills of the Cotswolds, to flat, marsh country around Glastonbury. Or in two hours you could drive from the chalk cliffs of the south coast looking toward France, to the rolling downs and the wooded Weald of Sussex and Kent, and on to the center of London, one of the largest cities in the world. Writers have drawn inspiration from those landscapes for hundreds of years, and simply to be there links us to them and to their creations.

I am sure that you will have a warm welcome, whichever of these sites you visit: children's literature brings out the best in people!

Peter Hunt
Professor of Children's Literature
Cardiff University

Acknowledgments

I wrote this book in the solitude of my office, but I did the research in the company of my wife, Nancy Northcott, and our son, Gavin West. To visit the sites described in these pages, we crisscrossed Great Britain, driving more than 3,000 miles in our various rental cars. I would have never found many of the sites that we visited if it were not for Nancy's excellent navigation skills. I would not have noticed as many details if it were not for Gavin's keen eyes. I thank them both for their help and for their enthusiasm.

I also received assistance from other people. Peter and Sarah Hunt hosted a lovely tea for us during our most recent visit to Britain. After tea, Peter and I talked at length about my research, and he helped me better understand the significance of some of the sites on my itinerary. Kara Keeling provided me with useful information on C. S. Lewis and his connections to the Holy Trinity Church in Headington Quarry. Tina Hanlon helped me with my entry on Philippa Pearce, Paula Connolly supplied information on A. A. Milne, and Angelica Carpenter told me about the connections between E. Nesbit and the Crystal Palace Park. Greg Wickliff provided me with valuable technical assistance while I prepared the manuscript for publication. During the course of our travels, innumerable docents and guides shared their insights with me. I never learned their names, but I remain indebted to them.

Finally, I gratefully acknowledge that this work was supported in part by funds provided by the University of North Carolina at Charlotte.

Introduction

Conducting the research for this book was one of the great pleasures in my career as a professor of children's literature. Summer after summer, my wife and I traveled across Great Britain, visiting sites related to British children's books or authors. On the last two trips, we took our son, Gavin, with us. His excited responses to the sites that we visited added to our enjoyment. I will always remember how much fun he had while playing Pooh sticks at the real Pooh Bridge or climbing around Tintagel Castle, wearing his King Arthur costume and brandishing his toy sword. I wanted to put off writing this book for about ten years so that I could continue my research. However, once I visited all the sites on my list, I knew, to paraphrase Lewis Carroll's Walrus, the time had come to write of many things.

My goal in writing *A Children's Literature Tour of Great Britain* is to help lovers of British children's literature go on their own literary pilgrimages. I therefore selected specific sites that are directly connected to British children's literature and that are now open to the public. I decided not to write about general regions, even though such regions do play important roles in many British children's books. Nor did I cover sites that require special permission to visit, such as the home that's featured in Lucy Boston's *The Children of Green Knowe*.

For the most part, this book is organized around authors. Each author entry begins with background information about the author, paying particular attention to the author's writings for children. I then provide detailed information about the site or sites associated with that author. For each site, I list the address, telephone number, and visiting hours. When dialing a British number from outside Great Britain, one should first dial 011 (the international access code) and then 44 (Great

Britain's country's code). One should then drop the zero from the prefix before dialing the remainder of the number. I also indicate if an admission fee is charged, although I do not list the actual fee since these fees change almost every year. In addition to the author entries, I include entries on a few sites that are related to children's literature but not to any particular author. These sites deal with the King Arthur legend and the Robin Hood legend.

Many of the sites covered in this guide appeal strongly to children. In a sense, these sites enable children to enter the pages of familiar children's books. They can pretend to be characters or interact with three-dimensional depictions of scenes from the stories. Even though such sites might seem too commercial or simplistic to adults, the pleasure that children have while touring these sites has a way of making the visits fun for the adults in the party.

Other sites covered in this guide appeal primarily to adult visitors. Such sites often feature display cases filled with rare books, artifacts related to an author's life, and lots of informative labels. During my visits to these sites, I often saw parents trying to read the labels while their children were tugging on their arms. I also saw restless children in some of the preserved homes of famous authors. Some children enjoy walking through Kipling's study and looking at his cluttered desk, but to many children Kipling's desk is just another desk.

I value equally the sites the are geared to children and the sites that are intended for adults. As the father of a 9-year-old boy, I enjoyed hiking through Sherwood Forest, pretending to be the evil sheriff, while my son, also known as Robin Hood, kept robbing me. As a professor of children's literature, I enjoyed examining the displays about Thomas Hughes in the Tom Brown's School Museum, even though my son was ready to play hooky after half an hour. However, I understand that not everyone has such eclectic tastes when it comes to literary sites. For this reason, I indicate in my entries if particular sites are especially appropriate for a certain age group.

Although the readers of this guide might not want to visit every one of the sites that are covered, I found something of interest at each one. In my opinion, they are all worth investigating, for all can provide visitors with a better understanding and deeper appreciation of British children's literature.

1
King Arthur

How the legendary King Arthur went from being a sixth-century chieftain to the subject of numerous children's books is a long and complex tale, involving a creative intermingling of fact and fancy. Serious historians dismiss as fiction much of the legend that has grown up around King Arthur. Most historians, however, agree that the legend is at least partially based on a prominent warrior who helped lead the British resistance as the Saxons began invading southwestern Britain during the early decades of the sixth century.

The legend of King Arthur has its own history, which is a bit easier to document than the history of the actual man. The earliest written references to King Arthur can be found in Welsh texts from the late sixth century, but it took several more centuries before the legend took shape. In 1136, Geoffrey of Monmouth first outlined the legend as part of his *History of the Kings of Britain*. In the ensuing years, many other writers and poets spun off their own narratives about Arthur or the various characters associated with him, such as Merlin, Sir Lancelot, Queen Guinevere, and Sir Gawain. Sir Thomas Malory gathered together these various narrative threads and combined them in his classic work, *Le Morte d'Arthur*, which was published by William Caxton, the first English printer, in 1485.

The Arthurian legend initially came to be associated with children's literature in the mid-nineteenth century. Sir James T. Knowles led the way with his *The Story of King Arthur*, which came out in 1862. Within a few decades other children's versions of the legend appeared, such as Sidney Lanier's *The Boys' King Arthur* (1880), Henry Frith's *King Arthur and His Knights of the Round Table* (1884), Mary MacLeod's *The Book of King Arthur and His Noble Knights* (1900), and Howard Pyle's *King Arthur and His Knights* (1903). Of the more recent retellings of the legend for children, the two most prominent are T. H. White's *The Sword in the Stone* (1938) and Roger Lancelyn Green's *King Arthur and the Knights of the Round Table* (1957).

Although King Arthur's exploits are largely fictional, many of the places mentioned in the various retellings of the legend are real. In most cases historians cannot confirm the connections between the famous Arthurian sites and the real King Arthur, but that does not discourage lovers of the legend from visiting these sites. After all, many of these sites have been associated with King Arthur for over eight hundred years. Thus, even if the real Arthur never set foot in all of the sites associated with him, these places remain integral to the legend. There are dozens of Arthurian sites scattered across Britain, but the five sites described below are good places to begin an exploration of the world of the legendary King Arthur.

Tintagel Castle

Tintagel, Cornwall

According to the legend, Arthur was conceived and born in Tintagel Castle. The origins of this idea can be traced back to Geoffrey of Monmouth's *History of the Kings of Britain*, which he wrote almost 500 years after Arthur's estimated birth date. Most historians believe that Geoffrey of Monmouth had no factual evidence on which to base this claim, but the idea took root.

To the modern visitor the crumbling ruins of Tintagel Castle seem like the perfect place for the Arthurian legend to begin. Situated on a rocky crag overlooking the Atlantic, the castle has one of the most dramatic settings of any castle in Britain. Below the castle, where the sea meets the base of the crag, the forces of erosion have hollowed out a large cave, which is now called Merlin's Cave. The impressive ruins, dramatic setting, and intriguing cave all resonate with the story of Author's secret birth and his early connection to Merlin.

Most of the ruins that are now visible, however, are the remains of a medieval fortress built around 1230. Since Arthur was supposed to have been born about 473, the ruins we see today are not nearly old enough to be associated with Arthur. Fortunately for those who care about the plausibility of the legend, archaeologists have recently unearthed convincing evidence that the site upon which Tintagel Castle was built was a royal stronghold during the fifth and sixth centuries. Thus, even if there is no hard evidence that connects Arthur to Tintagel Castle, the site is at least old enough to have been his birthplace.

The connection between Arthur and Tintagel Castle goes unquestioned by the citizens and shopkeepers in the nearby village of Tintagel. In fact, the name of the village was changed in 1900 from Trevena to Tintagel to capitalize on the village's association with the castle. Also in 1900, the village saw the opening of King Arthur's Castle Hotel, which still caters to tourists who want to visit Tintagel Castle. Nowadays, the village is filled with shops and restaurants that play up the area's connection to King Arthur. One can purchase pewter figurines of the Knights of the Round Table or order an Excaliburger. To some visitors, the village's aggressive marketing of the King Arthur legend might seem a bit crass, but the actual castle remains sheltered from the commercialization of the legend.

Visitor Information:

Tintagel Castle is managed by English Heritage. It opens at 10 a.m. An admission fee is charged. For more information, contact:

> Tintagel Castle
> Tintagel, Cornwall
> PL34 0HL
> Tel: 01840 770328

Cadbury Castle

South Cadbury, Somerset

One of the great mysteries associated with the King Arthur legend is the whereabouts of Camelot. No existing castle or town in Britain bears the name Camelot. Thus, if it ever truly existed, it must have been abandoned long ago. The legend is so vague as to the location of Camelot that it is of little help to those seeking the site of Arthur's castle. Nevertheless, Arthurian scholars have devoted much effort to finding the location of the original Camelot. Over the centuries, numerous sites have been proposed, but the one that has the most credence among Arthurian scholars is Cadbury Castle, located near the tiny village of South Cadbury in the county of Somerset.

Apparently, the local residents have equated Cadbury Castle with Camelot for many centuries, but the first scholar to make this argument was the Tudor historian John Leland. In *Itinerary* (1542), he wrote, "At South Cadbyri standith Camallate, sumtyme a famose toun or castelle. The people can tell nothing thar but that they have hard say that Arture much resortid to Camalat." Since the 1950s, archaeologists have carried out extensive excavations at the site and have found evidence that Cadbury Castle served as the stronghold of a sixth-century chieftain. No evidence has been found to link the castle specifically to Arthur, but the history and location of the castle make it a plausible site for Arthur's Camelot.

Cadbury Castle is usually described as an Iron Age hill fort. It was built on the plateau of a large hill, the slopes of which are heavily wooded. Protected by four rings of earthworks, the fortified area consists of about eighteen acres.

Today visitors approach the site by following a footpath called Castle Lane. Once reaching the summit, visitors find themselves on a large meadow dotted with grazing cattle. There are no stone ruins, but the earthworks are clearly visible. If it is a clear day, visitors can see on the horizon the famous Glastonbury Tor, a large hill atop of which stands the remains of the medieval tower of St. Michael's Church. On the eastern slope is an ancient well, known as Arthur's Well.

Centuries ago Cadbury Castle must have hummed with activity, but today it is a quiet and isolated spot that invites visitors to indulge in a bit of reverie. It is the perfect place to contemplate the local legend about King Arthur. According to folklore, there is a hidden cave in the hill where Arthur is sleeping. On a certain night in June, Arthur awakes, and then he and his knights leave the cave and ride over the hill.

Visitor Information:

Cadbury Castle is located on private farmland, but there is open access during the day. There are signs in South Cadbury village indicating the exact location of the castle. A free car park is provided near the footpath, which leads to the site. The footpath leading up the hill is fairly steep and uneven, making it a difficult climb for visitors who are not comfortable hiking.

The Arthurian Centre

Slaughterbridge, Camelford

There are many different retellings of the legend of King Arthur, but most versions agree that King Arthur died in battle, fighting Mordred, his treacherous nephew. Arthur's final battle was fought, according to the legend, on the banks of the Camel River near the town of Camelford. The site of the battle is now known as either Slaughterbridge or the Camlann Battlesite.

Like many admirers of the King Arthur legend, the poet Alfred, Lord Tennyson, visited Slaughterbridge. He came in 1848, just as he was beginning to compose "The Idylls of the King," his famous series of poems based on the Arthurian legend. Tennyson had read a report of an ancient memorial stone, marking the spot of Arthur's death, although no one seemed to know exactly where the stone was located. Undeterred, Tennyson set out to find it. "Sought for King Arthur's Stone," he wrote, and "found it at last by a rock under two or three sycamores."

The Slaughterbridge Stone, as it is generally called, is over nine feet long. The Latin inscription clearly indicates that the stone was created as a memorial to a fallen leader, although scholars who have studied the inscription disagree as to whether the stone was intended to memorialize King Arthur. They agree, however, that the inscription dates the stone to the sixth century, which coincides with the time of Arthur.

In the mid-1990s, the Camlann Battlesite and the Slaughterbridge Stone were opened to the public as part of the newly created Arthurian Centre. Visitors can view the famous stone, take walks through the battle site, and examine the displays in a small museum devoted to the life and times of King Arthur. Detailed information about he history of the Slaughterbridge Stone is available in the museum. Rambunctious children can reenact King Arthur's final battle in the convenient play area, which includes a large wooden castle.

Visitor Information:

The Arthurian Centre is open seven days a week. Free parking and a tearoom are provided for visitors. An admission fee is charged. For more information, contact:

> The Arthurian Centre
> Slaughterbridge, Camelford
> North Cornwall
> PL32 9TT
> Tel: 01840 212450
> E-mail: camlann@arthur-online.com
> Website: www.arthur-online.com

Glastonbury Abbey

Glastonbury, Somerset

King Arthur is sometimes known as the Once and Future King, implying that he will come back from death and reassert his rule over Britain. This prophecy sounds a bit less incredible when one considers how restless he seems to have been since his final battle. His remains move around, depending on which version of the legend one is reading. Some early versions don't even acknowledge that he died; they say that he just went to sleep.

Even though there is no general agreement as to the location of King Arthur's grave, the most famous of the proposed sites is Glastonbury Abbey, once one of the wealthiest and most important monasteries in all of England. The argument that Arthur was buried on the grounds of the Abbey can be traced back to 1191. At the time, the Abbey was being rebuilt after a great fire in 1184. The monks, while excavating in the Abbey's burial ground, found a stone marker to which was attached a lead cross. The monks reported that the stone was inscribed with the words "Here lies buried the renowned King Arthur." The monks said that they then dug further down and found a coffin made out of a hollowed-out trunk of a tree. They claimed that the coffin contained not only the remains of King Arthur, but also those of his wife, Guinevere. In 1278, these remains were placed in a tomb near the High Altar of the Abbey church.

Glastonbury Abbey was dissolved during the reign of Henry VIII, after which the church, along with Arthur's tomb, fell into ruins. The exact location of the tomb was lost to history until it was rediscovered during an excavation conducted in 1934. The site was marked with a plaque, which can still be viewed by today's visitors. The plaque reads:

> Site of King Arthur's tomb. In the year 1191 the bodies of King Arthur and his Queen were said to have been found on the south side of the Lady Chapel. On the 19th of April 1278 their remains were removed in the presence of King Edward I and Queen Eleanor to a black marble tomb on this site. This tomb served until the dissolution of the Abbey in 1539.

Visitor Information:

Glastonbury Abbey is located on Magdalene Street in the city of Glastonbury. It opens daily at 9:30 a.m. An admission fee is charged. For more information, contact:

Glastonbury Abbey
Abbey Gatehouse
Magdalene Street
Glastonbury, Somerset
BA6 9EW
Tel: 01458 832267
E-mail: info@glastonburyabbey.com
Website: www.glastonburyabbey.com

King Arthur's Great Halls

Tintagel, Cornwall

Opened in 1933, King Arthur's Great Halls cannot claim any direct connection to the historic Arthur, but this site is perhaps the best place to visit if one wants to absorb the romance and grandeur associated with the legend. Frederick Thomas Glasscock, a wealthy businessman from London, conceived of the idea of creating an Arthurian museum after retiring to Tintagel in the early twentieth century. He did not want to build a stuffy museum, full of display cases and descriptive labels. Instead, he wanted to capture the atmosphere that he had long associated with the stories of King Arthur's Court. He accomplished this by constructing a building with two large halls modeled after the great halls found in medieval castles.

The first hall that Glasscock opened to the public is called either King Arthur's Hall or the Small Hall. Ten large paintings by William Hatherell are displayed on the walls. These paintings represent pivotal scenes from the Arthurian legend, beginning with his birth at Tintagel Castle and ending with his death at the hands of Mordred. The hall also features a dais upon which stands a throne for King Arthur. Visitors are free to sit on throne, since Arthur has yet to claim it.

The second hall, called the Hall of Chivalry, is larger than the first and boasts some of the finest stained glass windows in all of Britain. Created by Veronica Whall, the seventy-two windows celebrate the deeds of the various Knights of the Round Table. Also on display is a full-scale model of the Round Table around which visitors can stand and pretend to be one of Arthur's knights. A sculpture of the Sword in the Stone is on display as well, but it is mounted about fifteen feet above the floor, so visitors cannot try their hand at pulling out the sword.

This site also serves as the headquarters for the Fellowship of the Knights of the Round Table of King Arthur. The Fellowship provides lovers of the Arthurian legend with a sense of community. Members receive regular newsletters, free admission to the halls, and numerous other benefits.

Visitor Information:

King Arthur's Great Halls is open daily. In addition to the halls, visitors can browse through a large shop featuring Arthurian material. An admission fee is charged. For more information about the halls or the Fellowship of the Knights of the Round Table of King Arthur, contact:

King Arthur's Great Halls
Fore Street
Tintagel, Cornwall
PL34 0DA
Tel: 01840 770526

2
The Rev. W. Awdry and Christopher Awdry

The Rev. Wilbert Awdry (1916-1997) and his son, Christopher Awdry (1940-), are the authors of the famous Railway Series, featuring Thomas the Tank Engine and numerous other anthropomorphic steam locomotives. The Rev. W. Awdry began making up train stories for Christopher in 1942, while the then two-year-old boy was suffering from the measles. In an attempt to remember the details of the stories, the Rev. Awdry jotted the tales on scraps of paper. His wife repeatedly suggested that he try to get the stories published, so he submitted a few of them to a publisher named Edmund Ward. Ward liked the stories and published three of them in 1945 under the title *The Three Railway Engines*. Since this book sold reasonably well, Ward brought out Awdry's *Thomas the Tank Engine* in 1946, which was even more successful than the first book. Ward and Awdry then decided to produce a series, adding a new volume each year. After penning twenty-six books, the Rev. Awdry ended the series in 1973.

Christopher, who had never lost his childhood fascination with trains, decided to revive the series in 1983. Remaining true to his father's vision for the series, Christopher wrote in the style that his father had used and included many of the characters his father had created.

The Rev. W. Awdry set his books on an imaginary island that he named the Isle of Sodor. He situated this island in the North Sea between the Isle of Man and Lancashire. Sodor is not only set off physically from the rest of Britain, but also separated from the modernization of Britain that occurred after World War II. While steam locomotives gradually fell out of use in Britain in the postwar years, the mythical Isle of Sodor remained largely unaffected by this development.

The Rev. Awdry's love of steam locomotives led him to take an avid interest in the few isolated railways that still used these engines. One such line was the Ravenglass & Eskdale Railway, located in the Lake District. After visiting this unique railway, he decided to base a book on the engines that he had observed there. He titled the book *Small Railway Engines* (number twenty-two in the series), and it came out in 1967. Christopher also drew on the Ravenglass & Eskdale Railway in his 1990 book, *Jock the New Engine* (number thirty-four in the series).

The Ravenglass & Eskdale Railway

Ravenglass, Cumbria

The Ravenglass & Eskdale Railway, nicknamed La'al Ratty, started operating in 1875. At the time, this narrow-gauge railway was used primarily to haul iron ore from the Whitehaven Iron Mines in Eskdale to the town of Ravenglass, a distance of seven miles, where the ore was transferred to the trains running on the Furness Railway. In 1876 the Ravenglass & Eskdale Railway began to carry a limited number of passengers as well.

The railway struggled financially until 1915, when Waynne Bassett-Lowke purchased the railway and converted it into a passenger line, catering largely to tourists. Known throughout Great Britain for building miniature trains, Bassett-Lowke decided to use his miniature locomotives on this line. This decision meant that the track had to be converted to fifteen-inch gauge so that it could accommodate the tiny trains. The revamped railway carried passengers and goods for many decades, but in 1953 it was closed and put up for auction.

In 1960, a group of local business people formed the Ravenglass & Eskdale Railway Preservation Society and set out to raise the funds necessary to purchase the abandoned railway and convert it into one of the area's foremost tourist attractions. It took many years, but the Preservation Society accomplished its goal.

Today the Ravenglass & Eskdale Railway boasts a collection of eight miniature steam locomotives, several nonsteam locomotives, and a wide variety of passenger cars. It offers regular service between Ravenglass and Eskdale, with stops at four other stations. The station at Ravenglass features as a railway museum and a restaurant called The Ratty Arms.

Although the line runs through some beautiful countryside, it's the miniature steam locomotives that draw most people to the railway. This was certainly the case for the Rev. W. and Christopher Awdry. Both of these authors were so taken by these small engines that they included versions of these locomotives in their Railway Series.

In the Rev. W. Awdry's *Small Railway Engines*, there are three such engines: Rex, Bert, and Mike. These three are also included in Christopher Awdry's *Jock the New Engine*, but they are joined by a fourth named Jock. The man in charge of these small engines takes special pride in their abilities. At the conclusion of *Small Railway Engines*, he praises them for coping well with a minor accident. "Thanks to Rex," he says, "the accident did little harm. Bert and Mike worked like heroes, and our customers all admire the way we managed. They thought we were a 'toy railway,' but now they say we're Really Useful." In the context of the Railway Series, there is no higher compliment.

Visitor Information:

The Ravenglass & Eskdale Railway is open from the middle of February to the end of November. It is also open for about a week immediately after Christmas. Passengers usually board the train in Ravenglass. A round-trip journey takes approximately one hour and forty minutes. For information about the fares and the timetable, contact:

The Ravenglass & Eskdale Railway Co.
Ravenglass, Cumbria
CA18 1SW
Tel: 01229 717171
E-mail: rer@netcomuk.co.uk

3
Sir James M. Barrie

Born in the Scottish town of Kirriemuir, Sir James M. Barrie (1860-1937) is remembered today chiefly for his classic children's novel, *Peter Pan and Wendy* (1915), but during his lifetime Barrie was also well known for his plays and novels for adults. Barrie grew up in a large, working-class family. His father worked as a weaver of linen, but Barrie knew from an early age that he did not want to follow in his father's footsteps. Even as a child, he dreamed of making his living as a writer. His parents did their best to support his literary aspirations by making sure that he received a solid education. He completed his formal schooling in 1882, when the University of Edinburgh awarded him a master's degree.

After graduating, Barrie worked briefly as a journalist for the *Nottingham Journal* and then moved to London in 1885, where he supported himself as a freelance writer. He published several semi-fictionalized articles about his hometown of Kirriemuir, although he changed the name of the town to Thrums. He collected these pieces in two books: *Auld Licht Idylls*, published in 1888, and *A Window in Thrums*, published in 1889. In the 1890s, he turned much of his attention to drama, penning numerous plays for London theaters.

Throughout his writing career, Barrie often incorporated his real-life experiences in his books and plays. While most of his early works related to his Kirriemuir years, his story about Peter Pan was tied more to his life in London. After moving to London, he often took walks in Kensington Gardens, and during one of these walks he met the young sons of Arthur and Sylvia Llewlyn Davies. He soon became a friend of the family, and the Davies boys (George and Jack) came to regard Barrie as a sort of honorary uncle. Perhaps because he never had any children of his own, Barrie took an almost parental interest in the lives of these boys. In fact, after the boys' parents died, he was named the boys' legal guardian.

Early on in his relationship with these boys, he began telling them stories about Peter Pan. Barrie drew on this experience in an autobiographical novel titled *The Little White Bird* (1902). The central character is a boy named David, whom Barrie based on one of the Davies boys. In chapter 14 of the book, the narrator, who is based on Barrie, tells David a story about Peter Pan. A few years later, Barrie expanded on this story in a play titled *Peter Pan*, which was first performed in London in 1904. He then rewrote the story in the form of a full-length novel and published it under the title *Peter and Wendy* in 1911. Responding to complaints that the book was too long for children, Barrie shortened it and gave it the new title *Peter Pan and Wendy*. This shorter version, which came out in 1915, is the version that is generally read today.

Barrie's Birthplace

Kirriemuir, Scotland

In a biography of his mother, Barrie wrote, "Nothing that happens after we are twelve matters very much." Given Barrie's emphasis on the importance of childhood, he would no doubt agree that a visit to his birthplace is a good way to gain insights into his formative years.

The house in which he was born in 1860 was part of a complex of buildings known at the time as "The Tenements." Most of the residents, including Barrie's father, worked in Kirriemuir's linen industry. At the time of Barrie's birth, much of the downstairs portion of the house was set aside for his father's loom, and the family lived in the rooms above. While Barrie was still a toddler, his father moved his loom and other weaving equipment to a rented shop, and the family then used the space for a parlor. The Barrie family remained in this house until 1872, after which they moved to the other side of town. Since Barrie had already left home to attend boarding school when the family moved, their new home never meant very much to Barrie.

Once Barrie achieved fame, the citizens of Kirriemuir took pride that he was born in their town, but it wasn't until after Barrie's death in 1937 that his birthplace was opened to the public. A wealthy Barrie admirer named Duncan Elliot Alves purchased the house a few months after Barrie died and then donated it to the National Trust for Scotland, which continues to own and operate the property.

Nowadays, visitors to Barrie's Birthplace are treated to a variety of exhibits and modes of interpreting the house. The tour begins in the ground-floor parlor, which is now filled with memorabilia associated with Barrie. Items on exhibit in this room include original manuscripts, first editions of his works, and furnishings from his adult home in London. Two of the upstairs rooms—the kitchen and the bedroom—contain the same types of furniture and decorations that would have been used during the time of Barrie's childhood. The upstairs exhibition room takes a fanciful approach to Barrie's life and career. This room features a colorful diorama depicting Peter Pan flying through an open window, two original Peter Pan costumes from early productions of the play, and an electronic Tinkerbell that darts about the room.

Barrie's Birthplace also includes several interesting attractions outside the house. A separate washhouse is located a few yards from the main building. As a child, Barrie often played in this washhouse and even staged his first play in it when he was seven. As an adult, he used this washhouse as the inspiration for the little house that the Lost Boys built for Wendy in Never-Never Land.

Next to the washhouse is a small statue of Peter Pan created by Alistair Smart. The grounds also feature a delightful topiary, representing the crocodile from *Peter Pan*.

Visitor Information:

Barrie's Birthplace is open from the beginning of May to the end of September. There is an admission charge, but children under the age of five and members of the National Trust for Scotland are admitted free of charge. Visitors can also purchase beverages and snacks in an adjoining tearoom. For more information, contact:

Barrie's Birthplace
9 Brechin Road
Kirriemuir, Angus
DD8 4BX
Tel: 01575 72646

Peter Pan Statue

Kensington Gardens, London

Since Barrie's career as the creator of Peter Pan began as a result of his meeting the Davies boys while he was walking his dog through Kensington Gardens, Barrie always associated Kensington Gardens with Peter Pan. He wanted to share his special feelings about this place with others who had taken an interest in the story of Peter Pan, and he came up with a dramatic way to accomplish this goal.

Barrie commissioned the famous sculptor Sir George Frampton to create a large bronze sculpture of Peter Pan. Once the sculpture was completed, Barrie arranged to have it erected in Kensington Gardens. The installation of the sculpture took place in the middle of the night in April 1912, giving the impression that it appeared as if by magic.

The statue depicts Peter Pan playing his pipes atop an ornate column. The column is covered with animals and fairies, all seemingly mesmerized by Peter Pan's music. Near the base of the statue are several bronze rabbits that young children often attempt to kidnap.

Visitor Information:

The Peter Pan sculpture is located in Kensington Gardens on the western edge of the Long Water. Kensington Gardens, which adjoins Hyde Park, is in the center of London near the famous Kensington Palace. There is no admission charge to visit Kensington Gardens.

4
Michael Bond

Michael Bond (1926-) was working as a cameraman for the British Broadcasting Corporation during the mid-1950s, but he wanted to quit this job and become a full-time writer. He had already published some short pieces and was ready to try his hand at something more ambitious. He had an interest in writing fiction, but he initially had no plans to write for children. The origins of his career as a children's author can be traced back to the Christmas of 1957.

On Christmas Eve, he set out to do some last-minute shopping for his wife, Brenda. He went into a large department store on Oxford Street and wandered into the toy department. There he spotted a small toy bear sitting by itself on a shelf. It looked so forlorn that he impulsively bought it as a stocking stuffer. After he gave the bear to his wife, they decided to name it Paddington since their one-bedroom apartment was located near the Paddington railway station.

This toy captured Bond's imagination, and he decided to write a story about it. In the span of tens days, he dashed off his first children's book, which he titled *A Bear Called Paddington*. The British publisher William Collins Sons accepted the book and arranged to have Peggy Fortnum supply some illustrations. After the book came out in 1958, it became so popular that Bond went on to write many more books about this character, including *More About Paddington* (1959), *Paddington Helps Out* (1960), and *Paddington Abroad* (1961).

In the beginning of *A Bear Called Paddington*, Mr. and Mrs. Brown and their children, Jonathan and Judy, discover a bear sitting alone in the middle of Paddington station. A label attached to the bear reads, "Please look after this bear. Thank you." They are rather surprised when the bear speaks to them and even more surprised when the bear explains that he has just arrived from Peru. The Browns feel so sorry for the bear that they adopt him and give him the name Paddington. The rest of the book details Paddington's humorous adventures as he tries to fit into his new family. Disasters often follow in Paddington's wake, but he is such a good-natured bear that everyone quickly forgives him for the trouble he inadvertently makes. This pattern continues throughout the entire Paddington Bear series.

Paddington Station

London

One of the oldest of London's sixteen major train stations, Paddington Station can trace its origins back to the late 1830s when rail service was first introduced to London. The station as it appears today was completed in 1854. Designed by Isambard Brunel and M. D. Wyatt, Paddington Station is often cited as one of the best surviving examples of ironwork architecture from the Victorian era.

The ceiling of Paddington Station is supported by massive iron arches, which soar above the heads of the bustling passengers. If one takes the time to look up, it is hard not to feel a bit dwarfed by the building. By setting the opening chapter of *A Bear Called Paddington* in Paddington Station, Bond accentuates the sense of awe and isolation that Paddington experiences as he sits on his battered suitcase waiting for someone to befriend him.

Current visitors to Paddington Station can see a sculpture of Paddington Bear near one of the escalators in the center of the station. The sculpture is directly based on the illustration that Peggy Fortnum supplied for the first page of *A Bear Called Paddington*. Just as in the Fortnum illustration, the sculpture depicts Paddington sitting atop a battered suitcase. He is wearing a broad-brimmed hat, and around his neck is a string to which is attached a tag that reads, "Please look after this bear. Thank you."

Most of the passengers in the train station hardly notice the sculpture as they rush to catch their trains, but for those who take the time to stop and look, the sculpture often sparks an emotional reaction.

Whether he is a toy on a shelf, a character in a book, or a sculpture in a train station, Paddington Bear has a special ability to tug at our heartstrings.

Visitor Information:

Paddington Station is located on the corner of Eastbourne Terrace and Pread Street. The station serves as the nucleus for the Paddington/Bayswater neighborhood. Like London's other major train stations, Paddington Station is always open. There is no admission charge. For more information about Paddington Station and the other train stations operated by Railtrack, contact:

Railtrack PLC
Railtrack House
Euston Square
London
NW1 2EE
Tel: 020 7557 8000
Website: www.railtrack.co.uk

5
Frances Hodgson Burnett

It can be argued that Frances Hodgson Burnett (1849-1924) was both a British and an American author. She was born in Manchester, England, where she spent her childhood. Her father, a wealthy ironmonger, died when Frances was three, and the family fortunes steadily declined after his death. In 1865, her mother moved the family to Knoxville, Tennessee, at the invitation of a relative who ran a grocery store there.

Shortly after moving to America, Frances began her writing career, selling her first stories while still a teenager. At the same time, she met a young man named Swan Burnett, and after a seven-year courtship, they were married. During the early years of her marriage, she wrote numerous short stories, novels, and plays, most of which she intended for women readers. Also during this period, she and her husband moved to Washington, D.C., where they raised their two sons, Lionel and Vivian.

Burnett's career as a children's author began in 1885 with the publication of *Little Lord Fauntleroy*, a story about an American boy who moves to England upon learning that he is the grandson of an English earl. This novel became a best-seller in both America and Great Britain.

Her next important children's book was *Sara Crewe*, which first came out in 1888. Based on the fairy tale Cinderella, this book features a wealthy girl who attends Miss Minchin's Select Seminary for Young Ladies in London. Initially, she is treated well, but when the headmistress learns that the girl's father has died penniless, the girl is forced to become an exploited servant. An expanded version of this story was published in 1905 under the title *A Little Princess*.

The most enduring of Burnett's children's books proved to be *The Secret Garden*, which appeared in 1911. The central character in this story, an orphan named Mary Lennox, starts off as a self-centered snob who lives in India, but after moving to the Yorkshire moors, she gradually transforms into a caring child. Key to this change is her discovery of a secret walled garden that she begins tending.

A few years after the publication of *Little Lord Fauntleroy*, Burnett separated from her husband and began spending much of her time in Great Britain. From 1898 to 1907, she leased an old mansion called Maytham Hall, located near the village of Rolvenden in Kent. When her son Lionel became deathly ill in 1900, she returned to America to be with him, but after his death she moved back to Kent. She returned to America permanently in 1909. She built a home in Long Island, New York, and lived there until her death in 1924.

Great Maytham Hall

Rolvenden, Kent

The current structure known as Great Maytham Hall was built in 1910, but the original Maytham Hall was completed in the 1760s. There is considerable evidence that the original owners of the building and eighteen acres of surrounding grounds had ties to the smuggling business, which thrived in that part of Kent during the eighteenth century. During the nineteenth century, Maytham Hall went through a series of owners, and the building gradually decayed. In 1893, much of Maytham Hall burned. The owner repaired the part that remained standing and began leasing it out.

Frances Hodgson Burnett learned about the availability of Maytham Hall in 1898, and she visited it. Liking the place, she signed the lease. Shortly afterward, she wrote about it in a letter:

> It is a charming place with a nicely timbered part and a beautiful old walled kitchen garden. The house is excellent—panelled square hall, library, billiard room, morning room, smoking room, drawing room and dining rooms, 17 or 18 bedrooms, stables, two entrance lodges of the park and a square tower on the roof, from which we can see the English Channel.

Burnett especially liked the walled garden. Although this garden had not been properly tended for several years, the tangled rose bushes and unruly fruit trees appealed to her. She often set up a table and a chair in the garden and did her writing there. A rather tame robin also enjoyed the garden, and Burnett eventually coaxed the bird to eat from her hand.

The memory of Maytham Hall and the walled garden was fresh in Burnett's mind when she began writing *The Secret Garden* in 1909. She decided to set the book in the Yorkshire moors, partly because she had recently read Charlotte Brontë's *Jane Eyre*, and she liked how the moors figured in Brontë's story. However, she also wanted to include the walled garden from Maytham Hall, so she simply transplanted the garden, along with its resident robin, from Kent to Yorkshire.

The same year that Burnett began writing *The Secret Garden*, a man named H. J. Tennant purchased Maytham Hall and arranged to have the building completely rebuilt, but he left the old walled garden intact. From 1909 to 1936, the Tennants lived a life of luxury at Great Maytham Hall, but they sold the estate in 1936, and once again Maytham Hall went through a period of decline.

In the 1960s, the hall became a property of the organization now known as the Country Houses Association. The association converted part of the hall and the outbuildings into apartments for retirees. Several of the rooms and all of the gardens, however, have been opened to the public on a limited basis.

For visitors who are familiar with *The Secret Garden*, the walled garden is a particular treat. The garden is no longer the wild place that Burnett so lovingly described in *The Secret Garden*, but the old brick walls and the ivy-covered doorway still exert some of the "magic" that Burnett associated with this special place.

Visitor Information:

Great Maytham Hall is located just outside of the village of Rolvenden. It is open to the public from the start of May until the end of September on Wednesdays and Thursdays from 2:00 p.m. to 4:00 p.m. An admission fee is charged. For more information, contact:

Great Maytham Hall
Rolvenden, Kent
TN17 4NE
Tel: 01580 241346

6
Lewis Carroll

Lewis Carroll (1832-1898), the author of *Alice's Adventures in Wonderland* (1865) and its sequel, *Through the Looking-Glass and What Alice Found There* (1871), lived a paradoxical life. He possessed a wild imagination, but he followed rigid routines and organized every detail of his life. In his fiction, he lampooned the stuffiness of Victorian society, but his students thought of him as one of the stodgiest professors at Oxford University. He sent Alice on incredible adventures, but he seldom ventured away from his home. As a writer, he ranked among Britain's wittiest wordsmiths, but he found it difficult to speak to anyone but young girls. Although more is written about him than any other British children's author, he remains an enigmatic figure.

Carroll's real name was Charles Lutwidge Dodgson. He spent his early childhood in Daresbury, Cheshire, where is father served as a clergyman. There were eleven children in the family, and most of them were girls, which may help explain why he always enjoyed being around girls. As the eldest son, he was expected to follow in his father's footsteps and eventually become a clergyman. His parents sent him to Rugby School from 1846 to 1849 to prepare him to attend Christ Church College, which was his father's alma mater. Carroll, a quiet and introverted boy, felt out of place among the boisterous students at Rugby. In fact, he disliked nearly everything about the experience except his mathematics classes.

In 1851, he entered Christ Church College (one of numerous colleges that make up Oxford University), where he excelled in the study of mathematics. He also studied religion and eventually became an ordained deacon, but he never pursued a career as a clergyman in part because his serious stuttering problem interfered with his ability to conduct services.

After he graduated in 1854, the college appointed him sub-librarian, and few years later, he was offered a lectureship in mathematics, which he accepted. Since these positions included on-campus housing, Christ Church College functioned as his home as well as his place of employment.

About the same time that Carroll began his teaching career, the college hired Henry George Liddell as the new dean. Since Carroll lived near the deanery, he soon met Liddell's three daughters and one son. Carroll liked all of these children, but he especially liked Alice Liddell, the middle daughter. Carroll became a frequent visitor at the deanery and often participated in the children's outings.

On July 4, 1862, Carroll accompanied the Liddell girls on an afternoon boating trip, during which time he told the girls an extemporaneous story about Alice going on an underground adventure. The girls liked the story so much that Carroll decided to write it down. In 1863, he completed the manuscript, which he titled *Alice's Adventures Underground*, and gave it to Alice. He then set out to revise the story for publication. The expanded version, complete with illustrations by John Tenniel, came out in November 1865 under the new title *Alice's Adventures in Wonderland*.

Although the book received mixed reviews when it first appeared, it sold very well. Capitalizing on this success, Carroll wrote the sequel, *Through the Looking-Glass*, which Tenniel reluctantly agreed to illustrate. After several publication delays, it came out in December 1871, although it bore the date 1872.

Carroll went on to write a few other works for children, but they failed to match the success of his Alice books. In 1876, he brought out *The Hunting of the Snark*, a long nonsense poem published in book form. His last books for children were *Sylvie and Bruno* (1889) and *Sylvie and Bruno Concluded* (1893). These books deal with the experiences of two fairy children, but the plots are interrupted also by long passages on religion and morality.

Although Carroll felt disappointed over the public's lukewarm response to his books about Sylvie and Bruno, he continued to take satisfaction over the success of his Alice books. However, he never felt comfortable with his growing status as a celebrity among the literary set. As the years went on, he became increasingly crotchety. In fact, he often refused to answer to the name of Lewis Carroll, and he sometimes denied that he was the author of the Alice books.

Throughout his life, Carroll remained close to his sisters, several of whom lived in a house in Guildford. When he came down with a bronchial infection in December 1897, he went to Guildford to be with his sisters. He died on January 14, 1898, and his sisters arranged to have him buried in Guildford.

Christ Church College

Oxford

Christ Church College was founded in 1525 by Cardinal Wolsey, and was initially called Cardinal College. Following the English Reformation, Henry VIII refounded it as Christ Church College in 1546. Until the nineteenth century, its primary purpose had been to prepare men for the priesthood, but during the nineteenth century it gradually began broadening its educational offerings and became a bit more secular in its orientation.

Nowadays, Christ Church is an up-to-date educational institution with its own Website, but the physical campus looks much the same as it did when Carroll arrived there on January 24, 1851. The campus is organized around quadrangles. Carroll's first rooms were in the Peckwater Quadrangle, but he ultimately took up residence in the Tom Quad. The most notable architectural features on campus are Tom Tower, designed by Christopher Wren, and the Christ Church Cathedral, which serves as both the college chapel and the Cathedral of Oxford.

The campus of Christ Church is open to visitors, but tourists have access to only a few of the buildings. Visitors who are interested in Carroll should take the guided tour of the campus grounds. The guide points out the deanery where Alice Liddell lived, the corner rooms of Tom Quad where Carroll resided, and the library where Carroll's office was located.

Visitor Information:

Christ Church is open to visitors daily throughout the year. On Monday through Saturday, it is open from 9:30 a.m. to 6:00 p.m., and on Sunday from 12:45 p.m. to 5:30 p.m. An admission fee is charged. For more information, contact:

> Head Custodian
> Christ Church
> Oxford
> OX1 1DP
> Tel: 01865 267492
> Website: www.chch.ox.ac.uk

Alice's Shop

Oxford

Alice's Shop is located on St. Aldate's Street, opposite Christ Church College. During Carroll's years at Oxford, the shop sold groceries and other supplies. Alice Liddell often visited the shop, where she bought candy from the old woman who ran the shop. Knowing this, Carroll had the fictional Alice visit a version of the shop in *Through the Looking-Glass*. However, in his story, the shop has an unusual proprietor:

> [Alice] was in a little dark shop, leaning with her elbows on the counter, and opposite to her was an old Sheep, sitting in an arm-chair, knitting, and every now and then leaving off to look at her through a great pair of spectacles.

John Tenniel visited the shop and made sketches of it in preparation for doing the illustrations for the book. In his final illustrations, however, he reversed the position of the door and the window to make the pictures consistent with Carroll's use of mirror imagery in the book.

Today, Alice's Shop specializes in memorabilia related to Carroll's books. Visitors can buy books, chess sets, knickknacks, and candy.

Visitor Information:

Alice's Shop is located at 83 St. Aldate's Street. It is open on Monday, Tuesday, Thursday, and Friday from 10:00 a.m. to 4:30 p.m. and Saturday from 10:00 a.m. to 5:00 p.m. No admission fee is charged. For more information, contact:

Alice's Shop
83 St. Aldate's Street
Oxford
OX1 1RA
Tel: 01865 723793
E-mail: alice@sheepshop.com
Website: www.sheepshop.com

Guildford Museum

Guildford, Surrey

Carroll's association with the town of Guildford began shortly after his father's death in June 1868. Until that time, Carroll's six unmarried sisters had been living with their father at the Croft Rectory in Yorkshire, but their father's death meant that the Dodgson family had to leave the rectory. Since Carroll was now regarded as the new head of the family, it fell to him to find a home for his sisters. After looking for seven weeks, Carroll found a newly built home in Guildford that suited his sisters, and he purchased it for them. The house, which came to be known as The Chestnuts, served as his sisters' home until 1919.

Carroll frequently visited The Chestnuts. In his later years, he even occasionally preached at St. Mary's Church in Guildford. His final days were spent at The Chestnuts in the company of his sisters. They arranged to have him buried in Guildford's Old Mount Cemetery.

The Guildford Museum has a special exhibit related to Carroll and the Dodgson family. The exhibit features a copy of his diary and original letters written by Carroll. Various toys that belonged to the family are also on display, including a Looking Glass Box and the Wonderland Stamp Case. Nearby the museum are two statues of Alice. One depicts Alice watching the White Rabbit, and the other shows her passing through the looking-glass.

Visitor Information:

Guildford is located about twenty-five miles southwest of London. The Guildford Museum is adjacent to the Guildford Castle. In fact, the castle arch is incorporated into the museum. The entrance to the museum is just off Quarry Street. Guildford Museum is open Monday through Saturday from 11:00 a.m. to 5:00 p.m. No admission fee is charged. For more information, contact:

Guildford Museum
Castle Arch
Quarry Street
Guildford, Surrey
GU1 3SX
Tel: 01483 444750

Alice in Wonderland Centre

Llandudno, North Wales

Alice Liddell, the real girl upon whom Carroll's fictional Alice is based, was a frequent visitor to the Welsh town of Llandudno. The Liddell family often spent their summer holidays in the town. Initially they rented a house, but eventually the family acquired a plot of land on the West Shore of Llandudno and built a summer house, which they called Penmorfa. There is no hard evidence that Carroll ever visited the Liddell family during their summer holidays in Llandudno, but nevertheless many residents take pride in the town's association with Alice.

There are several landmarks in Llandudno that relate to Carroll. After Penmorfa was sold in the 1870s, it was transformed into the Gogarth Abbey Hotel, which has on display a painting of the "Walrus and the Carpenter" and a mural of the "Lobster Quadrille." In 1933, the town erected a statue of the White Rabbit. More recently, two residents, Muriel and Murray Ratcliffe, opened an attraction that they call the Alice in Wonderland Centre.

Opened in 1987, the Alice in Wonderland Centre features eleven life-size tableaux of scenes from *Alice's Adventures in Wonderland*. The center is entered through a gently sloping rabbit hole. Visitors are provided with individual headsets through which they can listen to relevant passages from Carroll's story. The models, many of which are animated, are based on Tenniel's illustrations. At the end of the twenty-minute tour, visitors are welcomed to browse in the Alice Curio Gift Shop.

Visitor Information:

The Alice in Wonderland Centre is located in Trinity Square just off the main Mostyn Street. The center opens daily at 10:00 a.m. An admission fee is charged. For more information, contact:

The Alice in Wonderland Centre
3 & 4 Trinity Square
Llandudno, North Wales
LL30 2PY
Tel: 01492 860082
E-mail: alice@wonderland.co.uk
Website: www.wonderland.co.uk

7
John Cunliffe

The children's authors most often associated with the Lake District are Beatrix Potter and Arthur Ransome, but John Cunliffe (1933-) needs to be added to the list. After working as a school librarian for several years, Cunliffe began writing children's books in the 1960s. His first children's book, *Farmer Barnes Buys a Pig*, came out in 1964. He went on to write several other books featuring Farmer Barnes, but it wasn't until he started his Postman Pat series in 1981 that his writing career took off. The Postman Pat stories served as the basis for a popular children's television program produced by the British Broadcasting Corporation. The stories were also released as picture books initially illustrated by Celia Berridge, and they quickly became best-sellers.

The Postman Pat books are set in a fictional town called Pencaster. Cunliffe, however, admits that this town is based on the real town of Kendal, where Cunliffe lives. Postman Pat delivers mail to the residents of Greendale Valley, which is based on Longsleddale, a valley north of Kendal. Pencaster is a bit smaller than Kendal, but both are quaint villages surrounded by gently rolling hills, which the locals refer to as fells.

In the Postman Pat books, Cunliffe celebrates the pleasures of village life. Cunliffe portrays Pencaster as an idyllic place where the residents take the time to talk with each other. Such is the case with Postman Pat. In the opening paragraph of *Postman Pat and the Treasure Hunt* (1981), the first book in the series, Cunliffe makes it clear that his central character does more than deliver the mail:

Pat is the Greendale postman. Everyday he drives his red van up the valley. Twisting along the twining roads; up and over hills, far away; down narrow lanes and tracks to farms and cottages. He brings letters and cards; newspapers and magazines; football-pools and catalogues and bills and birthday-cards and parcels full of who-knows-what? He also brings a smile, a joke, or a chat; news of the valley and who's-doing-what?

Museum of Lakeland Life

Kendal, Cumbria

The Museum of Lakeland Life focuses on the cultural history of the Lake District, with a particular emphasis on the town of Kendal. The museum has special exhibits on two children's authors who have Kendal connections: John Cunliffe and Arthur Ransome.

The John Cunliffe Room is as much a play area as it is an exhibit space. The room is filled with toys and puzzles based on the Postman Pat books. On the walls there are murals depicting scenes from the Postman Pat books as well as Cunliffe's Rosie and Jim books. Also on display are the original desk and typewriter that Cunliffe used when writing the Postman Pat series. Cunliffe donated these items in part because he wanted to give something back to the community from which he has drawn so much inspiration.

Visitor Information:

The Museum of Lakeland Life is adjacent to the Abbot Hall Art Gallery. These facilities are located at the southern end of Kendal, overlooked by Kendal Castle. The museum is open daily from 10:30 a.m. to 5:00 p.m. The museum is closed from late December until early February. An admission fee is charged. For more information, contact:

> Museum of Lakeland Life
> Abbot Hall
> Kendal, Cumbria
> LA9 5Al
> Tel: 01539 722464

E-mail: ws@lakelandmuseum.org.uk
Website: www.lakelandmuseum.org.uk

8
Roald Dahl

Roald Dahl (1916-1990) wrote some of the most popular children's books of the twentieth century, including *James and the Giant Peach* (1961), *Charlie and the Chocolate Factory* (1964), *Fantastic Mr. Fox* (1970), *The BFG* (1982), *The Witches* (1983), and *Matilda* (1988). His children's books achieved best-seller status not only in his native Great Britain but in many other countries as well.

Like his books, Dahl's life transcended national boundaries. He was born in South Wales, but both of his parents came from Norway. He spent many of his summer holidays visiting relatives in Norway, and he always took pride in his Scandinavian roots. A few years after graduating from Repton School in Derby, he moved to East Africa, where he worked for Shell Oil Company. His time in Africa made a deep impression on him, and he developed a lifelong interest in African wildlife. During the early years of World War II, he served as a fighter pilot for the Royal Air Force and was stationed in several Middle Eastern and Mediterranean countries. From 1942 through the 1950s, he spent much of his time in America, working first at the British embassy in Washington, D.C., and later in New York City as a freelance writer.

Dahl finally settled down in Great Missenden, a village located about thirty miles west of London in the county of Buckinghamshire. Dahl and his first wife, the famous actress Patricia Neal, purchased a farmhouse in Great Missenden in 1954, and they and their children spent their summers there for several years. In 1960, after their son was injured in an accident in New York City, they decided to make the house in Great Missenden their permanent home.

The house came with an apple orchard, and Dahl arranged to have a small brick garden shed built in the orchard. He found that the quietness of the shed was conducive to his writing. For the rest of his life, this tiny, often cold shed, cluttered with manuscripts, galleys, and files, was where Dahl went to write.

Dahl and Neal separated in 1979, but Dahl continued to live in Great Missenden. He married Felicity (Liccy) Crosland in 1983, and the house became her home, too.

The Roald Dahl Children's Gallery

Aylesbury, Buckinghamshire

Following Roald Dahl's death on November 23, 1990, his wife, Liccy Dahl, wanted to commemorate her husband's life in a way that reflected his gift for amusing children. She shared her thoughts on this matter with the administrators of the Buckinghamshire County Museum, located in the neighboring town of Aylesbury, and together they came up with the idea of creating a hands-on science museum that would incorporate elements from Dahl's children's books. On November 23, 1996, the Buckinghamshire County Museum opened its Roald Dahl Children's Gallery to much acclaim. The very next year the gallery won the Gulbenkian Award for being "the UK's best hands-on museum for children."

The gallery is located in a renovated coach house. Covering many of the walls are pictures by Quentin Blake, the British illustrator who provided the pictures for most of Dahl's books for children. Each of the interactive exhibits is based on a particular book by Dahl. For example, the exhibit that's designed around *James and the Giant Peach* features a giant peach that visitors can enter. Inside the peach are drawers full of insects that can be viewed through magnifying glasses. The exhibit designed around *Fantastic Mr. Fox* features a tunnel through which visitors can crawl and learn about the various things that are found underground.

Although most of the exhibits have a science connection, the exhibit associated with *Matilda* focuses on Dahl and his children's books. Called Matilda's Library, this exhibit includes copies of all of Dahl's children's books. Visitors can pick up phones and listen to Dahl reading selections from his stories. Visitors can also view a short video biography about Dahl.

Visitor Information:

The Roald Dahl Children's Gallery is part of the Buckinghamshire County Museum, which is located on Church Street in Aylesbury. The gallery caters primarily to school groups, which means that the general public cannot gain entrance when the British schools are in session. For the general public, the best times to visit are weekday afternoons from 3:00 p.m. to 5:00 p.m., Saturdays from 10:00 a.m. to 5:00 p.m., and Sundays from 2:00 p.m. to 5:00 p.m. Since the British schools are off for much of April and August, the gallery is open to the public from 10:00 am to 5:00 p.m. on most days during these two months. An admission fee is charged. Timed tickets are sold during peak times as the gallery only holds eighty-five people. These tickets are good for an hour visit, and entry is on the hour. For more information, contact:

The Roald Dahl Children's Gallery
Buckinghamshire County Museum
Church Street
Alyesbury, Buckinghamshire
HP20 2QP
Tel: 01296 331441
Website: www.buckscc.gov.uk/tourism/museum/

9
Ian Fleming

Ian Fleming (1908-1964) played many roles over the course of his eventful life. He worked as a journalist, banker, and spy. He traveled the world, collected fast cars, and played golf every chance he had. He created the fictional secret agent James Bond, one of the most famous characters in all of twentieth-century British literature, and wrote a dozen novels detailing Bond's adventures. Toward the end of his life, Fleming added one more role to his repertoire—children's author. He wrote only one children's book, *Chitty-Chitty-Bang-Bang* (1964), but this book went on to become nearly as popular as his spy thrillers.

Fleming began writing *Chitty-Chitty-Bang-Bang* in 1961, while recovering from a massive heart attack. An avid lover of sports cars, Fleming decided to focus his book on a magical car. This car, according to biographer Andrew Lycett, was "a composite of two cars Ian had known—his own breezy Standard which he had driven in Switzerland in the late 1920s, and a more traditional vintage sports car" that Fleming had seen at a race in the early 1920s. Fleming's magical car has the looks of a touring car from the 1920s. Fleming describes it in the book as a "twelve-cylinder, eight-liter, supercharged Paragon Panther." In addition to having a powerful engine, the car possesses other special qualities, including the abilities to fly, sail, and even reason.

A few years after Fleming's death, film producer Albert Broccoli, who made several of the James Bond movies, decided to make a film based on *Chitty-Chitty-Bang-Bang*. Ken Hughes served as the film's director, and Hughes and Roald Dahl coauthored the screenplay. The film version was released in 1968, and it starred Dick Van Dyke as Commander Caractacus Pott.

The screenwriters of the film version took many liberties with Fleming's original story. For example, the book is set during the early 1960s, but the film takes place around 1920. However, the magical car looks the same in both the book and the movie, and in both versions the car functions as the central character.

Cars of the Stars Motor Museum

Keswick, Cumbria

Keswick, a quaint village located in the heart of the Lake District, is home to a dentist and car collector named Peter D. Nelson. After one of his sports cars was used in a television production in 1982, Nelson became especially interested in collecting cars that had been featured in films or television programs. In 1989, he opened the Cars of the Stars Motor Museum and put his remarkable car collection on display.

The museum owns many of the cars used in the James Bond movies, two versions of the Batmobile, Laurel and Hardy's Model T Ford, and the Volkswagon Beetle used in one of Disney's Love Bug movies. It also features the Noddy car from the British Broadcasting Corporation's series based on Enid Blyton's Noddy books. However, the centerpiece of the museum, in Nelson's opinion, is the magical racing car from the film version of *Chitty-Chitty-Bang-Bang*.

During the production of the film, six versions of Chitty-Chitty-Bang-Bang were used, all of which were custom built by the Alan Mann Racing Company. So many versions were needed to accommodate the many transformations that the car undergoes over the course of the film. For example, a separate version was needed for the parts of the film in which the car turns into a hovercraft. Of the six cars that were built, two were destroyed while the film was in production.

Nelson managed to locate and buy two of the four surviving versions of the car. He owns the hovercraft car and also the main road car used in the film. It's the main road car that is on display in the museum. It still has its original engine and interior, and it still looks like it drove right out of the pages of Fleming's book. After seeing this remarkable car, visitors to the museum can easily understand why one of the children in Fleming's book says, "She's the most beautiful car in the world!"

Visitor Information:

The Cars of the Stars Motor Museum is located on Standish Street in the center of Keswick. The museum is open daily from 10:00 a.m. to 5:00 p.m. except during the winter months, when it keeps more limited hours. An admission fee is charged. Visitors are not allowed to take photographs of the cars, but a souvenir booklet, which has photographs of most of the cars in the museum, is available for purchase. For more information contact:

> The Cars of the Stars Motor Museum
> Standish Street
> Keswick, Cumbria
> CA12 5LS
> Tel: 017687 73757
> E-mail: cotsmm@aol.com
> Website: www.cotsmm.com

10
Kenneth Grahame

Most children's authors write numerous books over their careers only to see their creations go out of print just a few years after being published. Kenneth Grahame (1859-1932) wrote only one children's book, *The Wind in the Willows* (1908), but it has never gone out of print. It received mixed reviews when it first came out, but over the years it has come to be regarded as one of the most important children's books written in the English language.

Grahame was born in Edinburgh, but he spent only a few years in Scotland. His mother died shortly before his fifth birthday, after which his father decided to send Kenneth and his siblings to live with their maternal grandmother in Cookham Dean, a small village near the River Thames in Berkshire. This move marked the beginning of Grahame's long association with the Thames and its peaceful riverbank. Throughout his childhood, he enjoyed exploring the river in a canoe or some other type of boat. He also enjoyed just sitting on the riverbank, listening to the gurgling water and observing the wildlife.

As he entered adulthood, Grahame gravitated toward a life of letters. He wanted to study literature at Oxford University, but his family could not afford to send him there. Instead, his relatives arranged for him to work as a clerk at the Bank of England. He excelled at this line of work and rapidly moved up the ladder. In 1898 he was named secretary of the bank, a remarkable accomplishment for a man his age. Despite his success as a banker, however, he never truly enjoyed working for the Bank of England. Nor did he ever give up on his earlier ambition to have a literary career. He tended to associate with writers and intellectuals, and he began writing stories and essays during his spare time. These writings were collected in three books: *Pagan Papers* (1893), *The Golden Age* (1895), and *Dream Days* (1898).

Grahame lived the life of a bachelor until just before his fortieth birthday. In July 1899, he married Elspeth Thompson. About a year later, their only child, a boy they named Alastair, was born. Married life did not especially agree with Grahame, but he took great pleasure in being a father. While Alastair was still little, Grahame spent hours telling the boy stories that he would create as he went along. These stories featured anthropomorphic moles, water rats, and other animals. In May 1907, Alastair was scheduled to go on a holiday with his governess, but he did not want to miss his father's bedtime stories, so Grahame agreed to send Alastair a letter each day in which he would write down a story. Later that year, Grahame used these letters as the basis for *The Wind in the Willows*.

The year 1908 not only saw the publication of *The Wind in the Willows*, but also marked the end of Grahame's career as a banker. He resigned his position and moved his family back to Cookham Dean in part because he wanted once again to live near the Thames. Some years later they moved to the nearby village of Blewbury, and eventually they settled in Pangbourne, another village located along banks of the Thames.

Although Grahame enjoyed being so close to his beloved river, his life was far from happy. His marriage continued to deteriorate. He was also troubled by Alastair's inability to cope with school. The boy briefly attended both Rugby and Eton, but he had to withdraw from them because he was too depressed to concentrate on his studies. He eventually enrolled in Christ Church College at Oxford, but after two years he died. His death might have been an accident, but the evidence suggested that he committed suicide.

Grahame became something of a recluse during his final years, but he still took pleasure in talking about *The Wind in the Willows* and its four central characters: Mole, Rat, Toad, and Badger. He was pleased when Ernest H. Shepard agreed to do the illustrations for a new edition of the book. In 1930 he met with Shepard, and during the meeting he talked about the book's characters. As Shepard later recalled in an article published in *The Horn Book*, Grahame concluded their talk by saying, "I love these little people; be kind to them."

Grahame died on July 6, 1932. He was buried near his son in St. Cross Churchyard in Oxford. The epitaph on his headstone reads, "To the beautiful memory of Kenneth Grahame, husband of Elspeth and father of Alastair, who passed the River on the 6th July 1932, leaving childhood and literature through him the more blest for all time."

Thames Rivercruise

Reading, Berkshire

The River Thames begins in the Cotswolds at Trewsbury Mead and flows west for about 200 miles until it merges with the North Sea near the Isle of Grain. Grahame was especially familiar with the forty-mile stretch of the river between Pangbourne, where he spent his final years, and Cookham Dean, where he spent much of his childhood. This stretch of the Thames served as the inspiration for the setting of *The Wind in the Willows*. Although Grahame's beloved riverbank has changed much since his death in 1932, there are still some undeveloped areas along the river that Grahame would recognize.

One of the best ways for visitors to appreciate Grahame's passion for the Thames is to take a cruise along the river. Thames Rivercruise, a business based in Reading, offers a cruise that provides visitors with a delightful introduction to the riverbank community that so inspired Grahame. This particular cruise runs between Reading and Mapledurham House.

Passengers depart from the Thameside Promenade at Caversham. The first part of the cruise goes through Reading. Here the banks of the river are lined with expensive houses almost all of which were built after Grahame's death. Once the boat leaves Reading, however, the riverbanks are lined with trees, just as they were in Grahame's time. Observant passengers can occasionally spot wildlife at the river's edge. There are several small islands along the way that are reminiscent of Pan's Island from *The Wind in the Willows*. The cruise ends at Mapledurham House, the Elizabethan manor house that likely served as the model for Toad Hall. The round-trip takes about two hours, but most passengers carry away memories that last for a lifetime.

Visitor Information:

Thames Rivercruise offers a variety of summer river cruises on weekends and bank holidays. The cruise to Mapledurham House departs from the Thameside Promenade at Caversham at 2:00 p.m. and arrives at Mapledurham House about forty-five minutes later. At this point passengers have two options. They may stay on the boat and return to Reading, or they may get off the boat and take a two-hour tour of the Mapledurham Estate, after which they can board the boat for the return trip. The cruise to Mapledurham House is available from the end of April to the end of September. A fee is charged. For more information, contact:

> Thames Rivercruise
> Pipers Island, Bridge Street
> Caversham
> Reading, Berkshire
> RG4 8AH
> Tel: 01189 481088
> Website: www.thamesrivercruise.co.uk

Mapledurham House

Mapledurham, Oxfordshire

Readers of *The Wind in the Willows* are introduced to Toad Hall in the chapter titled "The Open Road." Mole, who has never before seen Toad Hall, and Rat approach the grand house by boat:

> Rounding a bend in the river, they came in sight of a handsome, dignified old house of mellowed red brick, with well-kept lawns reaching down to the water's edge. "There's Toad Hall," said the Rat. . . . "Toad is rather rich, you know, and this is really one of the nicest houses in these parts, though we never admit as much to Toad."

Grahame's description of Toad Hall perfectly matches the appearance of Mapledurham House, an Elizabethan manor house situated beside the Thames. Most scholars who have studied the origins of *The Wind in the Willows* believe that Grahame based Toad Hall on Mapledurham House. In fact, when Grahame met with Ernest Shepard to discuss Shepard's illustrations for the book, the author suggested that Shepard model his pictures of Toad Hall after Mapledurham House, and the illustrator did just that.

Sir Michael Blount began construction on the current Mapledurham House in 1588, and the house was finally completed in 1612. Throughout its long history, Mapledurham House has remained in the Blount family. Visitors to the house can view a large collection of pictures and family portraits dating between the sixteenth and eighteenth centuries. A high point for many visitors is the great oak staircase that features the original Tudor woodwork.

On the grounds of the estate there is a working water mill that still produces stone-ground flour. There are also picnic tables set up near the water mill where visitors can eat while watching the Thames flow by. With a little imagination, one can easily picture Rat and Mole sprawled on the grass feasting on their picnic of "coldtonguecoldhamcoldbeefpickledgherkinssaladfrenchrollscresssandwidgespottedmeat."

Visitor Information:

Mapledurham House is located about four miles northwest of Reading on the north bank of the Thames. It is open to the public on Saturdays, Sundays, and bank holiday Mondays from Easter to the end of September. The opening times are from 2:00 p.m. to 5:30 p.m. An admission fee is charged. For more information, contact:

Mapledurham House,
The Estate Office
Mapledurham, Reading
RG4 7TR
Tel: 01189 723350
Website: www.henley-on-thames.org.uk/out/maple.htm

The Wind in the Willows Attraction

Rowsley, Derbyshire

The pages of *The Wind in the Willows* are filled with detailed descriptions of some very inviting places. Many a reader has felt drawn to the pastoral splendor of the riverbank or longed to enter the cozy homes of the central characters. Although it is not possible to enter Grahame's book in a physical sense, the creators of The Wind in the Willows Attraction have provided visitors with the next best thing. Using techniques developed by theater designers, the artists and technicians who built The Wind in the Willows Attraction created a series of elaborate dioramas depicting pivotal scenes from the book. Each diorama is based on one of the pictures that Ernest Shepard did when he illustrated the book.

Visitors to The Wind in the Willows Attraction first enter a small theater where they watch a short film about Grahame's life and his classic story. They then wander down a winding trail along which the dioramas are arranged in an order that parallels the book's plot. Special sound and light effects are used throughout the attraction, and some of the dioramas even make use of specially created aromas. Child visitors especially like the diorama that depicts that events in chapter 2, which is titled "The Open Road." The centerpiece of this diorama is Toad's gypsy caravan. Children can actually enter the canary yellow caravan and pretend to prepare a snack in the small kitchen that's inside.

Once visitors have viewed all of the dioramas, they come to a small nature museum called the Wide World. This part of the attraction features several displays about the animals and plants that are associated with riverbanks, meadows, and woods. A short film, titled *Toad's Tale*, is shown in this area. This film provides factual information about the lives of real toads, moles, water rats, and badgers.

Visitor Information:

The Wind in the Willows Attraction is located in Peak Village, a large complex of shops, eating places, and arts and crafts studios. The Wind in the Willows Attraction is open daily except Christmas and New Year's Day. An admission fee is charged. For more information, contact:

> The Wind in the Willows Attraction
> Peak Village
> Rowsley, Derbyshire
> DE4 2NP
> Tel: 01629 733433
> E-mail: toad@hop-skip-jump.com

11
Thomas Hughes

When Thomas Hughes (1822-1896) wrote *Tom Brown's Schooldays* (1857), he not only launched his own career as an author, but also laid the foundation for an entire genre. Although Hughes was not the first British author to write a school story for children, he more than anyone else defined the form of the British school story.

Hughes spent his early childhood in the village of Uffington, near the famous Vale of the White Horse, which is a prehistoric figure of a horse cut into the chalk hillside. He greatly enjoyed roaming the village and playing rough-and-tumble games with the local boys. In 1834, his father decided to send him to Rugby, a boarding school for boys. Rugby's headmaster at the time was Thomas Arnold, and Hughes soon developed a strong admiration for Arnold. Hughes largely enjoyed his days at Rugby, even though he did not excel in his studies. He had much more success in the area of athletics. In his final year at Rugby, he served as the captain of both the rugby football team and the cricket team. Hughes went on to Oxford and eventually became a lawyer.

Hughes married Frances Ford in 1847, and before long they had several children. Since Hughes had such positive memories from his days at Rugby, he and his wife believed that their eldest son, Maurice, should go to Rugby, too. Their son, however, felt uneasy about going away to school. In an attempt to prepare Maurice for life at Rugby, Hughes spent much of the summer of 1856 writing a semifictionalized account of his school days, which he shared with his 8-year-old son.

A friend saw the manuscript and suggested that Hughes submit it for publication. Hughes followed his friend's advice, and sent several of the early chapters to a publisher named Alexander Macmillan. Macmillan liked what he read and agreed to publish the book as soon as Hughes finished writing it. In the meantime, however, Hughes's eldest daughter became deathly ill with scarlet fever. It wasn't until after his daughter's death that Hughes completed the manuscript. *Tom Brown's Schooldays* came out in the spring of 1857, and it quickly achieved commercial and critical success. It went through five printings in its first year. By 1890 nearly fifty printings of the book had been published.

Literary critics praised *Tom Brown's Schooldays* for providing one of the first realistic accounts of British school life. On the whole, life at Rugby is presented in a positive light in the pages of Hughes's novel, but the unpleasant aspects are not ignored. For example, Tom Brown has several encounters with a bully named Harry Flashman. Critics also praised Hughes for creating a fully developed central character whose gradual maturation is consistent with the experiences of real schoolboys. In the beginning of the book, Tom Brown is a carefree boy who prefers sports and pranks over books and lessons. By the end of the story, Tom has become a responsible and studious young man.

Hughes went on to write several other autobiographical novels, including *The Scouring of the White Horse* (1858), which grew out of his early childhood in Uffington, and *Tom Brown at Oxford* (1861), which related to his own experiences at Oriel College in Oxford. Neither of these books, however, came close to matching the success of *Tom Brown's Schooldays*. During the final decades of his life, Hughes switched his emphasis from writing to politics. He became very involved in Christian Socialism and devoted much of his time to promoting various idealistic causes. He died of heart failure on March 22, 1896, and was buried at Brighton on England's south coast.

In the years since Hughes's death, *Tom Brown's Schooldays* has continued to attract attention and influence writers. A silent film version was released in 1916, and two other prominent film versions were released in 1939 and 1951. In 1969, George MacDonald Fraser published the first of a series of novels featuring Harry Flashman, the bully from Hughes's novel, although in Fraser's novels Flashman is older. The influence of *Tom Brown's Schooldays* can also be seen in J. K. Rowling's Harry Potter series. Some critics argue that the character of Harry Potter has much in common with Tom Brown. Similarly, the headmaster in the Potter books, a wizard named Albus Dumbledore, is very similar to the headmaster in Hughes's novel.

Tom Brown's School Museum

Uffington, Oxfordshire

The opening chapters of *Tom Brown's Schooldays* take place in the village of Uffington. The book contains descriptions of several of the buildings in the village, including a small school. "The village was blessed," Hughes wrote, "with a well-endowed school. The building stood by itself, apart from the master's house, on an angle of ground where three roads met; an old grey stone building with a steep roof and mullioned windows."

Tom has a private tutor, so he does not attend this school, but most of his friends do. Since Tom wants to be with his friends, he begins lingering around the school, waiting for his friends to come out and play. On one such occasion, the door to the school is open, so Tom puts "his head into the school" and begins "making faces at the master when his head is turned." What follows is one of the more amusing scenes from the beginning of the book.

Built in 1617, this old stone structure still functioned as a school during Hughes's boyhood, but today the building is known as Tom Brown's School Museum. The museum includes a re-created Victorian schoolroom, material about the history of Uffington, and displays on the life and career of Thomas Hughes. The museum owns 136 different printings of *Tom Brown's Schooldays*, all of which are on display.

Tom Brown's School Museum is quite small, but anyone who visits the museum soon realizes that Thomas Hughes still has a big place in the hearts of Uffington's residents.

Visitor Information:

Located in the middle of Uffington village, Tom Brown's School Museum is adjacent to St. Mary's Church. The museum is open each weekend afternoon from Easter Sunday until the last full weekend of October. It opens its doors at 2:00 p.m. and closes at 5:00 p.m. A small admission fee is charged. For more information, contact:

Tom Brown's School Museum
Broad Street
Uffington, Oxfordshire
SN7 7RA

Tel: 01367 820259
E-mail: Tombrown@geocities.com
Website: www.geocities.com/Paris/Rue/1896

Rugby School Museum

Rugby, Warwickshire

When Thomas Hughes entered Rugby School in 1833, the school had already been in existence for over 250 years. Hughes arrived during Thomas Arnold's tenure as headmaster. This was a period of great change for the school. Under Arnold's leadership, Rugby became a bit more democratic, sports took on greater importance in the lives of students, and the curriculum began including science courses. Many of the changes that Arnold initiated have continued to shape the lives of Rugby's students right through to the present day. The campus, however, has changed a great deal since the days when Arnold was headmaster. A number of the older buildings were destroyed during the second half of the nineteenth century in order to make way for a series of buildings designed by a Victorian architect named William Butterfield.

As part of Rugby School's ongoing efforts to celebrate its long history, the school opened its own museum. Called the Rugby School Museum, it provides modern-day visitors with a good understanding of what it was like to be a student at Rugby during the nineteenth century. The display includes actual desktops on which boys from long ago carved their names. The museum also includes information on Thomas Hughes and extensive material on the history of Rugby, the famous sport that originated at the school in 1823.

Visitors who want to see the campus can take a guided tour, which leaves from the museum each day at 2:30 p.m. Visitors who are especially interested in Hughes should be sure to see the statue of Hughes located near the school library.

Visitor Information:

The Rugby School Museum is located on Little Church Street in Rugby. It is open daily, but on Sundays it is open only in the afternoon. An admission fee is charged. For more information, contact:

Rugby School Museum
10 Little Church Street
Rugby, Warkwickshire
CV21 3AW
Tel: 01788 556109
E-mail: Museum@rugby-school.warwks.sch.uk

12
Charles Kingsley

Charles Kingsley (1819-1875) was a clergyman, social reformer, poet, naturalist, and novelist. Of his many novels for adults, the most successful was *Westward Ho!* (1855). He also wrote several children's books, including *The Heroes* (1855), *The Water-Babies* (1863), and *Madam How and Lady Why* (1870). Of these, *The Water-Babies* has had the most lasting impact on British children's literature. He initially wrote *The Water-Babies* to please his youngest son, Grenville Arthur. Kingsley disliked the factual children's books that were popular in England at the time, and he set out to provide his son with a wholesome fantasy story as a sort of antidote to all of the children's books that stressed facts and figures.

In the process of writing *The Water-Babies*, Kingsley drew on many of his interests and experiences. Like most of his fellow members of the Christian Socialist movement, Kingsley opposed the use of child labor. He especially objected to the employment of children as chimney sweeps. He therefore used a young chimney sweep as the book's central character, and he devoted the first chapters to portraying the plight of these abused boys. The story's hero eventually drowns in a river, but instead of simply dying, he is transformed into an amphibious water-baby. For much of the book, the hero has underwater adventures involving fish and other types of marine life. In this portion of the book, Kingsley drew on the expertise that he had acquired while conducting the field research for a natural history book that he had published some years earlier titled *Glaucus; or, The Wonders of the Shore* (1855). In the conclusion of *The Water-Babies*, Kingsley made extensive use of his background as a clergyman. The final chapters are filled with religious symbolism, and the story ends with the hero going to heaven.

Toward the end of his life, Kingsley became affiliated with two of Britain's most prestigious institutions. He was appointed professor of modern history at Cambridge University, where he tutored the prince of Wales. He then became a canon of Westminster and served as chaplain to Queen Victoria. Although these positions were considered important honors during his lifetime, it is his contributions as a writer for which he is best remembered.

Clovelly Visitor Centre

Clovelly, Devon

For much of his childhood, Charles Kingsley lived in the ancient, cliffside fishing village of Clovelly, where his father was a parish priest. As a boy, Kingsley enjoyed walking down the steep cobbled street leading to the harbor. He then spent countless hours exploring the shore and watching the fishing boats. This experience stayed with him, and he drew on it when writing *The Water-Babies*.

Although Kingsley lived most of his adult life in Hampshire and Cambridge, he always had a special place in his heart for Clovelly. He visited Clovelly several times as an adult. In a letter written during one of these return visits, he wrote, "I cannot believe my eyes: the same place, the pavement, the same dear old smells, the dear old handsome loving faces again. It is as if I was a little boy again."

For many years, the residents of Clovelly have taken pride in the village's association with Kingsley. In 1994, the village paid homage to Kingsley by opening a special Kingsley Exhibition, which is administered by the Clovelly Visitor Centre. The exhibition consists of a re-creation of Kingsley's study, complete with a mannequin dressed in Victorian clothes. A second room features displays that provide information about Kingsley's association with the village and his writings.

Visitor Information:

Since Clovelly is closed to automobile traffic, visitors who arrive by car must park at the Clovelly Visitor Centre. From there they can take a short walk to the Kingsley Exhibition, which is housed in a restored building located in the middle of the village. The Kingsley Exhibition is open daily. An admission fee, which includes parking, is charged. However, there is no admission fee for children under the age of seven. For more information, contact:

Clovelly Visitor Centre
Clovelly, Devon
EX39 5SY
Tel: 01237 431781

13
Rudyard Kipling

Rudyard Kipling (1865-1936) always identified himself as an Englishman, but for much of his life there was no place in England that he could truly call home. During his childhood he felt much closer ties to India, where he was born and spent the first six years of his life, than he did to England, where he endured eleven unhappy years attending boarding schools. When he decided to become a writer, Kipling returned to India and worked as a journalist for several years. After marrying an American woman named Caroline (known as Carrie) Balestier in 1892, he moved with his bride to her hometown in Vermont. There Kipling wrote *The Jungle Book* (1894), *The Second Jungle Book* (1895), and *Captains Courageous* (1897). The Kiplings' first two children, Josephine and Elsie, were born during this period.

Kipling and his family moved to England in 1896, and the next year they settled in Rottingdean, a village on the Sussex Downs a few miles from Brighton. They rented a house called The Elms, and this house is where he wrote *Stalky & Co.* (1899), *Kim* (1901), and *Just So Stories for Little Children* (1902). While living in Rottingdean, the Kiplings had a son whom they named John. Unfortunately, a few years after the birth of John, their daughter Josephine died.

In 1902 the Kiplings bought a seventeenth-century house called Bateman's. Located near the village of Burwash, Bateman's became Kipling's permanent home. He wrote two children's books during his years at Bateman's: *Puck of Pook's Hill* (1904) and *Rewards and Fairies* (1910). As several of Kipling's biographers have pointed out, the first decade that Kipling spent at Bateman's was the happiest time in his life. He had a basic faith in progress during this period. It seemed to him that his family, his career, and his country were all progressing in positive directions.

Following the outbreak of World War I, Kipling lost his sense that all was right with the world. He felt a tremendous antipathy toward Germany and strongly supported Great Britain's involvement in the war. It pleased him when his son, John, joined up to fight in 1914, but the pride he took in his son's patriotism and valor did little to assuage the grief he felt after John was killed at the Battle of Loos in October 1915.

After his son's death, Kipling sank into a depression that he never fully overcame. His feelings of grief were combined with his sense of bitterness concerning the gradual collapse of the British Empire. During his final years, Kipling lived a fairly isolated existence at Bateman's. He still took some pleasure in writing, but none of his works from this period attracted much attention. During his final years, he worked on his autobiography, *Something of Myself* (1937), but this book did not appear until after his death. Kipling died on January 18, 1936.

The Grange

Rottingdean, East Sussex

Operated by the Rottingdean Preservation Society, the Grange is an art gallery and museum that focuses on the history of East Sussex and its past residents. Since Kipling was one of Rottingdean's most famous residents, the Grange has a special room that is devoted to Kipling and his Rottingdean years.

The centerpiece of the Kipling Room is a life-size model of Kipling sitting in a reconstruction of his study in The Elms, the rented house where he and his family lived from 1897 to 1902. The model is based on a portrait of Kipling that was painted in 1899. The Kipling Room also includes displays on Kipling's life and writings. In another section of the room, there are displayed ten prints by Maurice and Edward Detmold. These pictures were used to illustrate a 1908 edition of *The Jungle Book*.

The Elms is within easy walking distance from the Grange. Although The Elms is not open to the public, visitors can read a commemorative plaque that the Kipling Society placed upon the garden wall.

Visitor Information:

The Grange is located on the Green in the middle of Rottingdean. It is open daily from 10:00 a.m. to 4:00 p.m., except on Sunday, when it is open from 2:00 p.m. to 4:00 p.m. Admission is free. For more information, contact:

> The Grange
> The Green
> Rottingdean, East Sussex
> BN2 7HA
> Tel: 01273 301004

Bateman's

Burwash, East Sussex

In September 1902, Kipling and his family moved into Bateman's, a seventeenth-century manor house that Kipling had purchased for £9,300. Constructed of local sandstone, Bateman's was completed in 1634. Although many people had owned the house before Kipling purchased it, no one had tampered with the house's basic architectural style. This authenticity greatly pleased Kipling. He and his wife decided that they would not make any renovations that would alter the essential character of the house. The only major change they made was to bring in electricity, but they made sure that the wires leading to the house were buried.

Kipling's love of the house carried over to the surrounding grounds. The house came with 33 acres, but Kipling decided that he wanted an even bigger estate. He therefore bought a neighboring farm, an old water-powered mill, and an adjoining tract of land. With these purchases, the estate grew to 300 acres.

Kipling put much money and effort into improving the gardens near the house. He added paths, a rose garden, and a concrete-lined pond in which his children often played. When he won the Nobel Prize for Literature in 1907, he spent most of the prize money on the gardens.

Living at Bateman's prompted Kipling to take an interest in the history and geography of the region. He soon worked this interest into his writings. He began working on a series of stories in which two children, whom he modeled after Elsie and John, learn about exciting events that occurred at various points in English history. He used the countryside around Bateman's as the setting for most of these stories, although a few of them take place in other parts of Great Britain. In 1904, he published these stories in a book titled *Puck of Pook's Hill*. A second collection called *Rewards and Fairies* came out in 1910.

Following Kipling's death in 1936, his wife, Carrie, decided to leave Bateman's to the National Trust. She died three years after her husband's death, and not long after that Bateman's was opened to the public. For readers of Kipling's books, there are several rooms that are particularly noteworthy. Lovers of *The Jungle Book* and *The Second Jungle Book* should be sure to see the small inner hall on the ground floor, which contains three plaster reliefs depicting scenes from the books. These reliefs were created by Kipling's father. In the exhibition room, located upstairs in what was once the Kiplings' guest bedroom, there are many fascinating documents related to Kipling's literary career. The most interesting room is Kipling's study upstairs. This room, with its book-lined walls, is just as it was when Kipling last used it. His desk, which measures ten feet in length, remains cluttered with the trinkets and talismans that he had collected on his travels.

To understand fully what Bateman's meant to Kipling, visitors need to tour the gardens and grounds, since it was here that Kipling turned for inspiration. The National Trust keeps the outdoor areas looking much the same as they did during Kipling's time. The formal garden still has a manicured look, and the informal garden continues to resemble a meadow in bloom. The pond and streams in which Elsie and John waded look just as inviting as ever. After spending an hour wandering through the gardens and down the shaded paths, visitors can easily see why Kipling so deeply loved this place.

Visitor Information:

Bateman's is about one mile west of Burwash on A265. It is open from 11:00 a.m. to 5:30 p.m. on Monday, Tuesday, Wednesday, Saturday, and Sunday. It is closed from November to March. An admission fee is charged. For more information, contact:

Bateman's
Burwash
Etchingham, East Sussex
TN19 7DS
Tel: 01435 882302

14
Edward Lear

In 1832, Edward Lear (1812-1888) left his native London to take up residence in Knowsley Hall, a country manor not far from Liverpool. He was hired by the owner of the manor, Lord Edward Stanley, to make drawings of Stanley's private collection of animals. Stanley had seen the illustrations that Lear had already completed of the parrots in the London Zoo, and Stanley thought that Lear would be the perfect person to draw the animals in his menagerie.

From 1832 to 1837, Lear spent his days creating pictures of Stanley's animals, but during the evenings Lear often visited Stanley's grandchildren, who lived in the manor. He sometimes wrote a poem for them that he would illustrate with a humorous sketch. He invariably wrote limericks, a verse form he adopted as his own after a friend introduced him to a limerick about an "Old Man of Tobago" who lived on "rice gruel and sago." Lear wrote his limericks one or two at a time over a period of several years. He wrote them only to delight the children, and he had no plans to publish them. The limericks eventually circulated throughout the household, and even the adults seemed to enjoy them. It pleased Lear that his limericks were popular, but he continued to think of himself as an artist, not as a poet.

Upon finishing his work for Stanley, Lear decided to make his living as a landscape artist. For the next several years, he traveled throughout Italy and a number of other European countries, producing many picturesque canvases. He returned to England in 1845 to oversee the publication of three of his books, all of which were brought out during the following year. As he saw it, the most important of these was *Illustrated Excursions in Italy*. The other two stemmed from work he had done a decade earlier. One, titled *Gleanings from the Menagerie and Aviary at Knowsley Hall*, contained the drawings that Lord Stanley had commissioned, and the other, titled *A Book of Nonsense*, consisted of his limericks and their accompanying drawings.

It is not clear why Lear finally decided to publish these limericks. The children for whom Lear originally wrote them must have urged him to do so, and undoubtedly several of Lear's friends concurred. Whatever the reason, Lear seemed to have some doubts about the wisdom of publishing his poems, for he refused to publish the book under his name, a practice he did not follow with any of his other books. His use of the word "nonsense" was also indicative of Lear's ambivalence. As Emile Cammaerts pointed out in *The Poetry of Nonsense*, "Lear chose this word as an humble disparagement of his poems and as a plea for the public's indulgence." Lear, however, soon discovered that he had no reason to worry. The book became a critical and commercial success, and has since come to be seen as a classic children's book.

The response to his book gratified Lear, but it did not convince him to become a full-time writer of nonsense. He continued to devote most of his time to traveling, painting, and drawing. Still, he remained interested in nonsense and often included nonsense writing in his letters to friends. In 1861, he released an enlarged edition of *A Book of Nonsense*, and this time he published it under his own name. In the 1870s, Lear finally brought out some new books of nonsense poetry. He published *Nonsense Songs, Stories, Botany and Alphabets* in 1871, *More Nonsense* in 1872, and *Laughable Lyrics* in 1877. *More Nonsense* consisted of limericks, but the other two books contained some longer poems, such as "The Owl and the Pussy-Cat" and "The Jumblies." When he died on January 29, 1888, Lear was already more famous for his poetry than his paintings. Nowadays, he and Lewis Carroll are widely recognized as Britain's foremost creators of nonsense poetry.

London Zoo

Regent's Park, London

While still a teenager, Edward Lear began working as a zoological draughtsman for the Zoological Society of London. The society created and maintained a zoological garden at Regent's Park, and it was here that Lear went to observe the birds that he intended to draw. He contributed several drawings for the society's guidebook titled *The Gardens and Menagerie of the Zoological Society Delineated* (1830). He then set to work on an illustrated book featuring the society's parrot collection. Titled *Illustrations of the Family of Psittacidae, or Parrots*, the book initially appeared in parts between 1830 and 1832.

The pictures of birds that Lear did for the London Zoological Society not only launched his career as professional artist, but also provided him with material that he would later use in his nonsense poetry. Throughout his life he remained interested in birds, and he included birds in many of his poems. One of his most famous limericks is about an old man whose beard becomes the nesting place for "Two Owls and a Hen, four Larks and a Wren." An owl also appears in his masterpiece "The Owl and the Pussy-Cat."

The Zoological Gardens where Lear spent so many hours during his teenage years still exists, but today it is called the London Zoo. In Lear's day, only scientists and members of the Zoological Society could visit the site. In 1847, however, the zoo opened its doors to the public.

The zoo still has a fine collection of parrots, many of which are housed in the Macaw Aviary. Built in 1994, the Macaw Aviary is large enough for the macaws to fly and select their own mates. In addition to parrots, the zoo also has a special exhibit of water birds and cranes and a large aviary known as the Bird House. Visitors who spend much time watching the birds of the London Zoo can began to appreciate Lear's lifelong love of these feathered creatures.

Lear never married, but in a letter written to a friend he once playfully suggested that he would like to marry a bird. "I think of marrying some domestic henbird," he wrote, "and then building a nest in one of my own olive trees, where I should only descend at remote intervals during the rest of my life."

Visitor Information:

The London Zoo is located on the north side of Regent's Park. The zoo is open every day except Christmas. From November through February, it is open from 10:00 a.m. until 4:00 p.m. From March through October, it is open from 10:00 a.m. until 5:30 p.m. An admission fee is charged. For more information, contact:

The London Zoo
Outer Circle
Regent's Park, London
NW1 4RY
Tel: 020-7722 3333
Website: www.londonzoo.co.uk

Knowsley Safari Park

Prescot, Merseyside

The origins of Knowsley Safari Park can be traced back to the private menagerie founded by Lord Edward Stanley, the thirteenth earl of Derby. For Stanley, collecting animals was not just a hobby. He saw himself as a zoologist, and he often studied the specimens in his collection. He even served as president of the Zoological Society of London. In this capacity, he met Edward Lear.

When Stanley offered Lear the opportunity to draw pictures of the animals and birds in Stanley's menagerie, the two men were at opposite ends of several spectrums. Stanley was a wealthy nobleman in his late fifties, whereas Lear was a poor commoner in his early twenties. Nevertheless, their mutual interest in animals served as a basis for a friendship that lasted until Stanley's death in 1851.

After the death of the thirteenth earl of Derby, his menagerie stayed in the family. For many years, members of the family and their friends enjoyed viewing this large collection of unusual animals and birds, but members of the public were not allowed to visit. In July 1971, the eighteenth earl of Derby decided to open to collection to the public. However, instead of opening a traditional zoo, he created a drive-through safari park in which the animals roamed free. Initially, visitors drove along a three-mile course from which they could see lions, cheetahs, monkeys, giraffes, zebras, elephants, and antelopes. A few years later, the route was expanded to five miles, and visitors could see more animals, including camels, buffaloes, rhinos, and tigers.

Knowsley Safari Park has evolved into one of Merseyside's most popular tourist attractions. In addition to its collection of animals, it features several amusement park rides, a gift shop, picnic areas, and a restaurant in which the décor is based on African art and wildlife.

If Lear were to visit Knowsley Safari Park today, he probably would not recognize it as the place where he worked for several years. However, he surely would appreciate the amusing role reversal of having the humans caged in their cars while the beasts wander about freely.

Visitor Information:

The Knowsley Safari Park is located a few miles northeast of Liverpool. It is open daily from the first of March to the end of October. Its hours of operation are from 10:00 a.m. until 5:30 p.m. An admission fee is charged. For more information, contact:

Knowsley Safari Park
Prescot, Merseyside
L34 4AN
Tel: 0151 430 9009
E-mail: safari.park@knowsley.com
Website: www.knowsley.com

Edward Lear Hotel

Marble Arch, London

Although Edward Lear grew up in London, he never created a permanent home for himself in London during his adult years. His natural wanderlust led him to spend much of his time traveling, and he often painted landscapes of the places that he visited. Almost every year, however, he returned to London for a few months to sell his paintings and to visit with friends and family. He usually rented a flat that would be large enough for him to exhibit a year's worth of paintings.

From 1857 through 1859, Lear rented a building just north of Marble Arch, and he lived there during his visits to London. At the time, the address for this building was No. 16 Upper Seymour Street. In the letters that he wrote while living at this address, Lear playfully changed the name of the street to "Hupper Seemore Street." In more recent years, the name of the street has been shortened to Seymour Street. The numbering system has also been changed. As a result, the current address of the building that Lear rented is 30 Seymour Street.

Lear's residence on Seymour Street is now the Edward Lear Hotel. In addition to naming the hotel after Lear, the hotel's management celebrates Lear in other ways as well. Examples of Lear's landscapes and bird pictures are on exhibit in the hotel's reception area. The hot plates used in the breakfast room are decorated with Lear's limericks. The hotel owns a first edition of Lear's *A Journal of a Landscape Painter in Calabria*, and guests are allowed to view the book.

Lear, like the duck in his poem titled "The Duck and the Kangaroo," longed "to go out in the world beyond." Thus, it is fitting that his name is attached to a business that caters to travelers.

Visitor Information:

The Edward Lear Hotel is a moderately priced hotel located one block from Marble Arch. It's also near Oxford Street and Hyde Park. The hotel has thirty-one rooms, twelve of which have their own bathrooms. The room rates vary, but all include a traditional English breakfast. For more information, contact:

Edward Lear Hotel
30 Seymour Street, Marble Arch
London
W1H 5WD
Tel: 0171-402 5401
E-mail: reception@edlear.com
Website: www.edlear.com

15
C. S. Lewis

Clive Staples Lewis (1898-1963) is remembered in the world of children's literature for *The Lion, the Witch, and the Wardrobe* (1950) and the other six books that comprise his Chronicles of Narnia. He also, however, wrote works of theology, including *The Pilgrim's Regress* (1933) and *The Screwtape Letters* (1942), works of science fiction, including *Out of the Silent Planet* (1938) and *Perelandra* (1943), and several works of literary scholarship.

Although born in Belfast, Ireland, Lewis was educated in England. He generally disliked school, but he loved literature, especially the fantasy novels by George MacDonald. He entered Oxford University in April 1917 with the intention of studying literature and philosophy, but he left a few months later to enlist in the British Army. He served in the military during World War I and was wounded during the Battle of Arras. In 1919 he resumed his education at Oxford and eventually completed his degree in July 1923.

After graduating, Lewis began teaching English language and literature at Magdalen College, one of the twenty-eight colleges that make up Oxford University. He continued to teach at Oxford until 1954, when he accepted a teaching position at Cambridge University.

During most of his Oxford years, he lived in a house called the Kilns, which he and his brother, Warren (Warnie) Lewis, purchased in 1930. Located in a community on the outskirts of Oxford known as Headington Quarry, the Kilns was so called because it was built near several kilns that had been used by a local brickworks company.

Lewis formed a friendship with J. R. R. Tolkien in the late 1920s. Both taught literature at Oxford and both had an interest in engaging in creative writing as well as conducting literary scholarship. The two often met at a local pub called The Eagle and Child, where they would discuss their various writing projects. (For more information about The Eagle and Child, see the Tolkien entry.) They often read and critiqued each other's manuscripts. After reading Tolkien's children's book titled *The Hobbit*, Lewis decided to try his hand at writing for children.

According to Lewis's biographer Roger Lancelyn Green, when Lewis showed Tolkien the first part of *The Lion, the Witch, and the Wardrobe*, Tolkien said that he "disliked it intensely." Tolkien felt that Lewis's book was too hastily written and that Lewis had not adequately developed the secondary world of Narnia. Lewis's publisher, however, had no such qualms. The book met with great success when it appeared in 1950, and the publisher encouraged Lewis to write sequels. Lewis had not intended to write other Narnia books, but he agreed to produce more. Even though it took Lewis just a few years to write the rest of the Narnia books, the publisher released the books at the rate of one per year. *Prince Caspian* came out in 1951, followed by *The Voyage of the Dawn Treader* (1952), *The Silver Chair* (1953), *The Horse and His Boy* (1954), *The Magician's Nephew* (1955), and *The Last Battle* (1956).

The Chronicles of Narnia grew out of Lewis's religious beliefs. Although Lewis turned away from religion during his youth, he embraced Christianity in 1931, and from then on he incorporated religion into most of his writings. The series, for example, features a great lion named Aslan, who is clearly a Christ figure. The Narnia books can be seen as examples of Christian allegory, but they also function as works of literature that stand on their own. In recognition of the books' literary merits, the British Library Association awarded the final book in the series, *The Last Battle*, the Carnegie Medal "for an outstanding book for children written in English" in 1956.

Holy Trinity Church

Headington Quarry, Oxford

When Lewis converted to Christianity in 1931, he marked the event by taking Communion in his parish church at Headington Quarry. Known as Holy Trinity Church, this church became the primary church that

Tintagle Castle, the birthplace of King Arthur, according to legend

Glastonbury Abbey, often thought to be the site of King Arthur's grave

King Arthur's Great Halls, located in Tintagle

One of the miniature steam engines used by the Ravenglass & Eskdale Railway

Barrie's Birthplace, located in Kirriemuir, Scotland

Peter Pan Statue, located in Kensington Gardens, London

Paddington Bear Statue, located in Paddington Station, London

Doorway to the walled garden featured in *The Secret Garden*

Christ Church College, part of Oxford University

Alice's Shop, located in Oxford

Museum of Lakeland Life, located in Kendal

Roald Dahl Children's Gallery, located in Aylesbury

Cars of the Stars Museum, located in Keswick

Thames Rivercruise, which departs from Reading

Mapledurham House, which served as the model for Toad Hall

Diorama of Rat and Mole boating, part of The Wind in the Willows Attraction in Rowsley

Tom Brown's School Museum, located in Uffington

Bateman's, Rudyard Kipling's home in Burwash

Parrot residing in the London Zoo

Edward Lear Hotel, located in London

Holy Trinity Church, located in Headington Quarry (photo by Kara Keeling)

Statue of Winnie, the bear that inspired Winnie-the-Pooh

Pooh Bridge, located in Ashdown Forest

Beatrix Potter's Hill Top Farm, located in Near Sawrey

Diorama from the World of Beatrix Potter Attraction, located in Bowness-on-Windermere

Captain Flint's boat, which in on display at the Windermere Steamboat Centre in Windermere

Statue of Robin Hood and Little John, located near the Sherwood Forest Visitor Centre

Hawes Inn, located in South Queensferry, Scotland

The Eagle and Child, located in Oxford

Lewis attended for the rest of his life. Even after he moved to Cambridge, he maintained close ties with this church. After his death on November 22, 1963, his funeral was held at Holy Trinity Church, and he was buried in the churchyard.

Built in the late 1840s, Holy Trinity Church had existed for over 100 years before Lewis joined the congregation. The members of the church welcomed Lewis as well as his brother, Warren Lewis, who joined at the same time. Once Lewis became a famous theologian, the members of the congregation felt honored that he attended their church.

Holy Trinity Church still celebrates its association with Lewis. There is a plaque in a pew off the north aisle, which indicates where Lewis and his brother used to sit. Near this pew, a Narnia window has been installed. The widow depicts Aslan the Lion and other features from the world of Narnia. The church carefully maintains Lewis s gravesite, with its distinctive gravestone. The words on the stone, which were composed by Warren Lewis, read as follows:

In loving memory of
My brother
CLIVE STAPLES LEWIS
Born in Belfast 29th November 1898
Died in this parish
22nd November 1963
Men must endure their going hence.

Visitor Information:

Holy Trinity Church is located on Quarry Road in the neighborhood of Headington Quarry, which is situated just inside the Oxford city ring road about two miles from Oxford city center. Like most churches in the area, Holy Trinity is kept locked when not in use, so the best day to visit the church is on Sunday. Sunday worship services are held at 8:00 a.m., 10:00 a.m., and 6:00 p.m. Access at other times can be arranged by telephoning the vicarage. The churchyard is always open to the public. For more information, contact:

Holy Trinity Church
Quarry Road
Headington Quarry, Oxford
OX3 8HN
Tel: 01865 762931

16
A. A. Milne

Children's authors often incorporate elements from their real lives in their fictional works for children, and such was the case for Alan Alexander Milne (1882-1956). In *Winnie-the-Pooh* (1926) and *The House at Pooh Corner* (1928), Milne incorporated his son, his son's toys, the name of a bear that his son liked to visit when they went to the London Zoo, and Ashdown Forest in Sussex, where the Milnes owned a vacation home. Even though Milne did not invent all of the elements that make up Pooh's magical world, he had a gift for making the real world seem like an enchanted place, at least within the pages of his books.

The son of a schoolmaster, Milne grew up in a household where education was valued. His education began at his father's school, but then he moved on to Westminster School, where he did especially well in his mathematics classes. In 1900, he entered Trinity College in Cambridge with the expectation that he would study mathematics, but he soon became much more interested in writing for a student periodical.

A few years after graduating from college, he found employment as the assistant editor of *Punch*, Britain's premier humor magazine. He worked at *Punch* from 1906 through 1914. During this period he married Daphne de Sélincourt because, he claimed, she laughed at his jokes. Following the outbreak of World War I, he left *Punch* and enlisted in the Royal Warwickshire Regiment.

Milne did not return to his job at *Punch* after the war. He became instead a full-time writer. At first he wrote mostly plays, but following the birth of his son, Christopher Robin, in 1920, Milne began writing poems and stories for children. He produced two collections of poetry for children: *When We Were Very Young* (1924) and *Now We Are Six* (1927). Both poetry collections proved popular, but it was for his Pooh books that he became most famous. The public wanted more Pooh books, but Milne decided to stop at two. Milne continued to publish new works, but the only one of his post-Pooh publications that enjoyed much success was his play *Toad of Toad Hall* (1929), which he based on Kenneth Grahame's *The Wind in the Willows*.

In his later years, Milne wrote primarily for adult readers. He did not like being labeled as an author of children's books, and he sometimes resented the fact that the reading public preferred his children's books to his novels and plays for adults. Nevertheless, when he wrote his autobiography, Milne expressed satisfaction in the success of his children's books. In his autobiography *It's Too Late Now* (1939), he provided a good explanation for why these books became so popular with children. His writing for children, he argued, "is the work of a . . . writer taking his job seriously even though he is taking it into the nursery. It seems that the nursery, more than any other room in the house, likes to be approached seriously."

London Zoo

Regent's Park, London

The real Christopher Robin enjoyed visiting the London Zoo, where his favorite animal was an American black bear named Winnie. The bear had been the mascot of Princess Pat's Canadian Regiment, but when the regiment joined the British forces at the outbreak of World War I, the officer in charge of the bear thought it best to leave Winnie in the care of the London Zoo. Winnie lived at the zoo from 1914 until her death in 1934.

In the introduction to *Winnie-the-Pooh*, Milne provided a humorous if somewhat fictional account of Christopher Robin's visits with the real Winnie:

> You can't be in London for long without going to the Zoo. There are some people who begin the Zoo in at the beginning, called WAYIN, and walk as quickly as they can past every cage until they get to the one called WAYOUT, but the nicest people go straight to the animal

they love the most, and stay there. So when Christopher Robin goes to the Zoo, he goes to where the Polar Bears are, and he whispers something to the third keeper from the left, and doors are unlocked, and we wander through dark passages and up steep stairs, until at last we come to the special cage, and the cage is opened, and out trots something brown and furry, and with a happy cry of "Oh, Bear!" Christopher Robin rushes into its arms.

Christopher Robin's affection for bears extended beyond Winnie. He had a teddy bear, whom he initially named Edward Bear, and Milne included this bear in one of the poems in *When We Were Very Young*. After Christopher Robin met Winnie, he decided to rename Edward Bear after Winnie as well as after a real swan that he called Pooh. He combined these names and came up with Winnie-the-Pooh.

When Christopher Robin visited the London Zoo, all of the bears were located in a large structure called Bear Mountain. Built in 1914, Bear Mountain was considered an ideal environment for bears at the time. In more recent years, however, the managers of the zoo determined that the enclosures were no longer suitable to house a large bear collection. The zoo therefore modified the structure to accommodate only sloth bears, which are native to the forests of India, Sri Lanka, and Nepal.

Even though Winnie died many years ago, the London Zoo still honors her memory. Winnie is mentioned in the zoo's official guidebook, and a statue of Winnie is located near Bear Mountain. The statue is just the right size for a child to hug.

Visitor Information:

The London Zoo is located on the north side of Regent's Park. The zoo is open every day except Christmas. From November through February, it is open from 10:00 a.m. until 4:00 p.m. From March through October, it is open from 10:00 a.m. until 5:30 p.m. An admission fee is charged. For more information, contact:

The London Zoo
Outer Circle
Regent's Park, London
NW1 4RY
Tel: 020-7722 3333
Website: www.londonzoo.co.uk

Ashdown Forest

Hartfield, East Sussex

In 1925, Milne purchased Cotchford Farm near the village of Hartfield. Located on the edge of Ashdown Forest, this farm became the family's vacation home. Christopher Robin was five years old at the time, and he immediately fell in love with the farm and the surrounding countryside. In his autobiography titled *The Enchanted Places*, he recalled his childhood passion for exploring the area:

> So there we were in 1925 with a cottage, a little bit of garden, a lot of jungle, two fields, a river, and then all the green, hilly countryside beyond—meadows and woods, waiting to be explored; and Nanny and I set out at once to explore them, bringing back reports of our discoveries.

Although Milne seldom accompanied his son on these explorations, he enjoyed hearing the boy's enthusiastic descriptions of the places where he and his nanny had their adventures. Many of Christopher Robin's favorite places in the forest soon found their way into Milne's two Pooh books. Not only did Milne describe the places in some detail, but the books' illustrator, E. H. Shepard, visited the Milnes and did on-site sketches of the spots mentioned in the books.

In the pages of the Pooh books, a densely wooded area known as the Five Hundred Acre Wood became the Hundred Acre Wood. An old quarry became Roo's Sandy Pit. A small wooden bridge called Posingford Bridge became Poohsticks Bridge. Gill's Lap, which is the official name for the highest point in the forest, became Galleon's Lap, which is where Pooh and Christopher Robin have their bittersweet parting in the last chapter of *The House at Pooh Corner*.

The house on Cotchford Farm is not open to the public, but the public can visit many of the sites that figure in the Pooh books. A good place to begin a Pooh pilgrimage is the Ashdown Forest Information Centre. In addition to providing visitors with information about the history of the forest and the wildlife that lives there, the Information Centre distributes a brochure that informs visitors where to find various Pooh sites.

The most popular of these sites is the Poohsticks Bridge. The bridge is a twenty-minute walk from the closest parking lot. It was at this bridge that Pooh is said to have invented the game of Poohsticks, in which the players drop sticks off one side of the bridge and then go to the other side to see whose stick is the first to emerge from under the bridge. Visitors who wish to play Poohsticks should be sure to gather sticks along the way, for there are very few sticks available near the bridge.

Another popular Pooh site is Gill's Lap (or Galleon's Lap, as it is called in *The House at Pooh Corner*), from which visitors have a panoramic view of Ashdown Forest. The A. A. Milne Memorial is located here. At the top of the hill, there is plaque set into a large rock. The words of the plaque read:

> And by and by they came to an enchanted place on the very top of the Forest called Galleon's Lap. Here at Gill's Lap are commemorated A. A. Milne (1882-1956) and E. H. Shepard (1879-1976) who collaborated in the creation of Winnie-the-Pooh and so captured the magic of Ashdown Forest and gave it to the world.

Visitor Information:

The Ashdown Forest Information Centre is situated one mile east of Wych Cross, where A22 meets A275. The center provides free parking and distributes brochures and maps that help visitors find the locations of the various sites that relate to Pooh. Most of the Pooh sites are located off of B2026. There are five car parks at different points along this road, each of which is near a particular Pooh site. The Ashdown Forest Information Centre and the various Pooh sites do not charge admission fees. The Information Centre is open from 11:00 a.m. to 5:00 p.m. on weekends and bank holidays and from 2:00 p.m. to 5:00 p.m. during summer weekdays. For more information, contact:

Ashdown Forest Information Centre
Wych Cross
Forest Row
Hartfield, East Sussex
TN7 4AE
Tel: 01342 823583
Website: www.ashdownforest.co.uk

Pooh Corner

Hartfield, East Sussex

Most of the places that Christopher Robin Milne described in his book *Enchanted Places* were located in Ashdown Forest. There was, however, a sweet shop in the village of Hartfield that he honored by including it in his memoir of the enchanted places of his childhood. As he recalled in his memoir, he often visited this shop with his nanny and a pet donkey named Jessica:

> Subsequent trips included our weekly visit to Hartfield, a mile away along a main road, up a steep hill, down a steep hill and in at the first shop on the left hand side. Jessica needed no urging and the woman behind the counter no instructions. It was a pennyworth of bullseyes for each of us.

The very same shop where Christopher Robin purchased candy as a child is now called Pooh Corner. Located in a building constructed over three hundred years ago, Pooh Corner stocks a large collection of Pooh books and memorabilia. It also sells bull's-eye candies similar to the ones that so appealed to the young Christopher Robin.

Visitor Information:

Pooh Corner is on High Street in Hartfield. It is open from 9:00 a.m. to 5:00 p.m. from Monday through Saturday. On Sundays and bank holidays, the shop is open from 11:00 a.m. to 5:00 p.m. between Easter and the end of October and from 1:30 p.m. to 5:00 p.m. the rest of the year. The shop is closed 25th and 26th December and New Year's Day. No admission fee is charged. For more information, contact:

> Pooh Corner
> High Street
> Hartfield, East Sussex
> TN7 4AE
> Tel: 01892 770456
> E-mail: shop@poohcorner.net
> Website: www.poohcorner.net

17
E. Nesbit

As a child, Edith Nesbit (1858-1924) exhibited a lively imagination, a tendency to disregard rules and conventions, a love of reading, and a curiosity about history. Although her teachers did not always appreciate this combination of traits, Nesbit resisted their efforts to mold her into a more conventional Victorian female. Her mother, who became a widow when Nesbit was just four, sent Nesbit to numerous boarding schools in the hopes of finding a school where her daughter would be happy but to no avail. Nesbit hated all of them. Instead of doing her schoolwork, she much preferred to read fantasy stories, play pretend games with her five siblings, or imagine herself living in some distant time. In her adult years, however, the same traits that characterized her childhood served her well when she began to write books for children.

In 1880, Nesbit married Hubert Bland, a brush manufacturer who would later become a journalist, and soon thereafter they started a family. A few years later, Bland caught smallpox and was no longer able to provide for the family, prompting Nesbit to turn to writing as a way to generate an income. At first she mostly wrote poems and short stories, but she eventually tried her hand at writing novels for children. Her first big success in this area was *The Story of the Treasure Seekers* (1899), in which six poverty-stricken siblings engage in various comical schemes to make money.

Nesbit did not include any fantasy elements in *The Story of the Treasure Seekers*, but magic figures prominently in most of the other children's books that she went on to write. Her fantasy books include

Five Children and It (1902), *The Phoenix and the Carpet* (1904), *The Story of the Amulet* (1906), *The Enchanted Castle* (1907), *The Magic City* (1910), and *Wet Magic* (1913). Among the fantasy elements found in these books are fantastic creatures, magical transformations, and time travel.

Not long after the publication of *Wet Magic* in 1913, Nesbit's life began to unravel. Her husband died in 1914. Even though their marriage had long been strained by numerous cases of infidelity, Nesbit had problems adjusting to life without Bland. For the next several years, she suffered from depression. She lost interest in writing for children, experienced difficulties managing her finances, and often felt overwhelmed by loneliness. She became less depressed after she remarried in 1917, but she never regained her interest in writing children's books. Her health began to deteriorate in 1922. She died on May 4, 1924.

Crystal Palace Park

Sydenham, London

In 1854, the famous Crystal Palace, a large iron-and-glass structure that had been used as the central building for the Great Exhibition of 1851, was moved from its original location in Hyde Park to Sydenham Hill in South London, where it would become a museum.

At the same time that the Crystal Palace was being moved and reassembled, a sculptor named Benjamin Waterhouse Hawkins created a series of twenty-nine life-size replicas of dinosaurs that he installed in a park near the Palace. Hawkins worked closely with Richard Owen, the first scientist to study dinosaurs. Together they designed the dinosaur sculptures to look as realistic as possible. Given the limited amount of information that was then known about dinosaurs, the sculptures were not always accurate. Nonetheless, these sculptures played an important role in the emerging field of paleontology, for they were the first replicas of dinosaurs ever built.

Nesbit visited the Crystal Palace as a child, and she was fascinated by the dinosaur sculptures. This experience marked the beginning of Nesbit's lifelong interest in prehistoric animals. She incorporated this interest into several of her fantasy books for children. For example, *Five Children and It* contains references to Megatheriums, Pterodactyls, Ichthyosaurus, and Plesiosaurus. In *The Magic City*, a prehistoric, giant sloth is mentioned.

The influence of Hawkins's dinosaur sculptures is especially evident in *The Enchanted Castle*. In this story, Hawkins's sculptures come alive at night. A character named Gerald is the first to witness this magical transformation:

> There was a crunching of the little stones in the gravel of the drive. Something enormously long and darkly grey came crawling towards him, slowly, heavily. The moon came out just in time to show its shape. It was one of those great lizards that you see at the Crystal Palace, made in stone, of the same awful size which they were millions of years ago when they were masters of the world, before Man was. . . . As it writhed past him he reached out a hand and touched the side of its gigantic tail. It was of stone. It had not "come alive" as he had fancied, but was alive in its stone.

Although Nesbit described the sculptures as being made of stone, the actual sculptures were not stone structures. Hawkins constructed iron skeletons for each of his dinosaurs. He built the foundations out of brick and used cement casts for the exterior surfaces. Since these sculptures were constructed out of durable materials, they survived their exposure to the elements fairly well. When the Crystal Palace was destroyed by fire on November 30, 1936, the dinosaur sculptures escaped unscathed. Time, however, finally took its toll on the sculptures.

The year 2001 marked a turning point in the history of Hawkin's dinosaur sculptures. Recognizing that the sculptures needed attention, the London Borough of Bromley, which owns Crystal Palace Park, embarked on a £3.6 million project to restore the sculptures. Work on the project began in the spring of 2001 and was completed in the fall of 2002. Also in 2001 a new picture book came out that features the sculptures. Titled *The Dinosaurs of Waterhouse Hawkins*, this book was written by Barbara Kerley and illustrated by Brian Selznick. In 2002 *The Dinosaurs of Waterhouse Hawkins* was recognized by the American Library Association as a Caldecott Honor Book for a "distinguished picture book for children."

Visitor Information:

Crystal Palace Park is located in southeast London near Sydenham. The park is open daily from 7:30 a.m. until dusk. No admission fee is charged. For more information, contact:

Crystal Palace Park Information Centre
Thicket Road
Penge
London
SE20 8DT
Tel: 020-8778 9612
Website: www.bromley.gov.uk

18
Philippa Pearce

Cambridgeshire has a special appeal for Philippa Pearce (1920-). She was born and grew up in the Cambridgeshire village of Great Shelford, where her father operated a mill located on the River Cam. After attending Perse Girls' School in the village, she enrolled in Girton College in nearby Cambridge, where she studied English literature and history. She graduated in 1942, after which she left Cambridgeshire to pursue a successful career as an editor and writer. In more recent years, however, she has returned to Great Shelford, the place that she has always thought of as her true home.

Pearce began writing books for children in the mid-1950s, and she has set most of them in Cambridgeshire. Such is the case with her most famous children's book, *Tom's Midnight Garden* (1958), which won the Carnegie Medal of the British Library Association "for an outstanding book for children written in English." Much of this time-travel story takes place in and around the same house where Pearce spent her childhood during the 1920s and early 1930s.

In the beginning of the novel, the year is 1958, and the house has been divided into flats. The central character, a boy named Tom Long, spends four weeks living in one of these flats with his Uncle Alan and his Aunt Gwen. During his first night in the flat, an old grandfather clock chimes thirteen times. Curious, he gets out of bed and begins exploring the house. He discovers a Victorian garden behind the house, which surprises him because the garden had not been there earlier that day. He eventually learns that this garden, which he can visit only at midnight, is a portal to an earlier time. When he goes back in time, he meets a girl named Hatty, and the two of them become friends.

Even though most of the book takes place in and around the garden, the book culminates with Tom and Hatty taking a skating trip down the river to the nearby town of Ely. Once they reach the town, they decide to visit the famous Ely Cathedral and climb to the top of the tower. It's during this point in the story that Tom's relationship with Hatty changes forever.

Tom's Midnight Garden is a fantasy story, but the well-drawn Cambridgeshire setting gives the book a sense of verisimilitude. Readers might not be able to enter Tom's magical midnight garden, but there are other places mentioned in the book that readers can visit, such as Ely Cathedral.

Ely Cathedral

Ely, Cambridgeshire

Located about sixteen miles north of Cambridge, the village of Ely is dominated by Ely Cathedral. The cathedral is the largest, oldest, and most visited building for miles around. The cathedral's origins can be traced back to a monastery founded on the site by Queen Etheldreda in the year 673. Work on the existing structure began in 1081 and was completed in 1118. In 1322, the cathedral's central tower collapsed, and Alan of Walsingham, a monk in Ely, designed a new tower to take its place. Built in the shape of an octagon, the new tower is much taller than the original square tower. The top of the octagon tower, which is called the Lantern, features several large glass windows that allow light to stream into the center of the cathedral.

Toward the end of *Tom's Midnight Garden*, Tom and his friend Hatty visit Ely Cathedral. They both feel moved upon entering this remarkable building:

> They walked through the town, making for the cathedral, and went in through the great west door. Inside, the failing of winter daylight was beginning to fill the vastness with gloom. Through this they walked down the nave towards the octagon; and it seemed to Tom as if the roof of the cathedral were like a lesser sky, for, although they walked steadily, when they looked upwards, they had moved very little in

relation to its spaces. Hatty walked with dazzled eyes: "Oh, I never thought there was anywhere so big—so beautiful!" she said.

While Tom and Hatty are exploring the cathedral, Tom notices a memorial tablet that captures his attention. The words on this tablet, which visitors can still see on a wall near the Lady Chapel, relate to Tom's desire to stop the passing of time. The tablet is dedicated to "Mr. Robinson, Gentleman of the City, who exchanged Time for Eternity on the 15th day of October one thousand eight hundred and twelve at the age of seventy-two." The phrase "Exchanged Time for Eternity" also intrigued Pearce when she saw the tablet while visiting the cathedral. In fact, this phrase helped inspire her to write *Tom's Midnight Garden*.

Visitor Information:

Ely Cathedral is located in the middle of Ely. It is open daily, but the hours vary depending on the season. From April through October, it is open from 7:00 a.m. to 7:00 p.m. From November through March, it is open from 7:30 a.m. to 6:00 p.m., except on Sundays, when it's open from 7:30 a.m. to 5:00 p.m. There is an admission charge, but children under the age of twelve are admitted free if accompanied by an adult. For more information, contact:

> Ely Cathedral
> Chapter House
> The College
> Ely, Cambridgeshire
> CB7 4DL
> Tel: 01353 667735
> E-mail: receptionist@cathedral.ely.anglican.org
> Website: http://cathedral.ely.anglican.org

19
Beatrix Potter

Beatrix Potter (1866-1943), the creator of *The Tale of Peter Rabbit* (1902) and many other picture books, did not see her career as a children's author as the primary focus of her entire adult life. She initially wanted to specialize in drawing scientific pictures of fungi, but when she failed to win recognition for her fungus pictures, she turned to picture books. Even though she achieved tremendous success in the field of children's literature, she eventually lost interest in the field and instead became a sheep raiser. Potter's desire to create picture books lasted for just a little over a decade, but the desire of children to read her books has continued unabated for a century.

Potter spent most of her childhood sequestered in the third-floor nursery of her parents' London home. Her parents required her to stay indoors and out of sight. Shortly after her birth, her parents hired a governess to raise her. She was educated at home in part because her parents did not approve of the children with whom she might come into contact at school. Nor did they allow other children to visit because they feared these children might introduce germs into the household.

Her father, Rupert Potter, had a strong interest in art, and he occasionally took his young daughter to art museums and galleries. He also purchased original artwork for her to enjoy, including a number of pieces by Randolph Caldecott, the famous illustrator of children's picture books. When she showed an interest in drawing and painting, her father hired a special tutor to teach her various artistic techniques.

During her lonely adolescence, Potter increasingly turned to the creation of art to express herself and give her life a sense of direction.

Besides art, the other main source of pleasure in young Potter's life was the family's summer vacations in the Lake District. The Potter family first visited the Lake District in 1882, and they so enjoyed their stay that they returned practically every summer thereafter. While in the Lake District, she spent her time exploring the outdoors, wandering through villages, drawing pictures of animals and plants, and attempting to domesticate rabbits, mice, and other small creatures that she managed to capture. In addition to brightening her early years, Potter's summer adventures helped shape her future life. As an adult, she remained interested in the ways of animals, the lifestyle of farmers and villagers, and the beauty of the Lake District.

Potter's parents impeded their daughter's transition to adulthood. They expected her to remain at home and help them run the household. They did not like the idea of her marrying, and they made it clear that only very wealthy suitors would have any chance of winning their approval. Thus, until Potter was a middle-aged woman, she continued to stay in the third-floor nursery except when she accompanied her parents on their summer visits to the Lake District.

Potter discovered that one way to escape from what she once called her "unloved birthplace" was through her art. She had long taken an interest in the often-overlooked beauty of wild mushrooms and other types of fungi, and she began doing detailed drawings of these organisms. Her interest in fungi led her to write an illustrated paper titled "On the Germination of Spores of Agaricineae," which she hoped to present before a group of professional botanists during a meeting scheduled to take place on April 1, 1897. The members of this organization, however, did not accept her paper.

Rebounding from the rejection of her fungi work, she decided to try her hand at writing and illustrating a picture book for children. Several years earlier she had written a letter to the son of one of her former governesses in which she told the tale of a rebellious young rabbit named Peter. She located this letter and expanded it into a picture book titled *The Tale of Peter Rabbit*. She submitted the book to a number of publishers. When none accepted it, she published it herself in 1901.

Soon thereafter Frederick Warne and Co. agreed to publish her story if Potter supplied color illustrations. She obliged, and Warne brought out the book in 1902. It was such a tremendous success that Warne eagerly published Potter's other children's books.

With the royalties that she earned from her first seven books, combined with a small inheritance that she had received, she was finally in a position to buy a home in her beloved Lake District. In November 1905, she bought Hill Top Farm, a working farm located a short distance from the town of Near Sawrey. The next year she had a new wing built onto the original farmhouse. She used the original part of the house for herself, while the man who ran the farm lived in the addition.

Potter longed to make Hill Top her primary residence, but she still felt compelled to continue living with her parents. Nevertheless, she spent a significant portion of each year living in her new home, and she began to use the property as the setting for her picture books.

Because she owned a farm in the Lake District, Potter became more and more involved in the day-to-day operations of her farm. Her interest in farming led her to purchase a second and somewhat bigger farm in 1909. Known as Castle Farm, this property adjoined Hill Top. A local solicitor named William Heelis helped Potter deal with the legal aspects of purchasing Castle Farm.

Potter and Heelis shared a strong attachment to the Lake District, and this mutual interest led them to become friends. Over the next few years, their friendship deepened. In 1912, Heelis asked Potter to marry him. Over the objections of her elderly parents, Potter accepted the proposal. Potter and Heelis were married in London on October 14, 1913, and from then on she preferred to be called Mrs. William Heelis.

Although the couple decided to make the house on Castle Farm their regular residence, Potter did not close her Hill Top house. She kept it furnished almost exactly as it had been before she married, but now it functioned primarily as her studio and study.

After her marriage, Potter lost interest in writing and illustrating children's books. Instead, she devoted her time and attention to her husband and to various agricultural pursuits, such as breeding Herdwick sheep. She also played an important role in the movement to preserve the Lake District's natural beauty and historic buildings. Potter continued to live happily in the Lake District until her death in 1943.

Hill Top Farm

Near Sawrey, Cumbria

From the moment she purchased Hill Top Farm in 1905 until her death in 1943, Beatrix Potter felt a special attachment to this seventeenth-century farmhouse and the surrounding property. The farm was the first place she ever thought of as her own, and she took great care in furnishing its rooms. She made sure that the house reflected her tastes and interests. Over the years, she came to think of Hill Top Farm as both a refuge and a source of inspiration.

Toward the end of her life, Potter decided to share this special place with the readers of her picture books. She therefore bequeathed the farm to the National Trust. In her will, she instructed the National Trust to keep the house in the condition that it was during her lifetime and to open the house to visitors. Three years after Potter's death, the National Trust began allowing the public to tour the house, and it has since become one of the Lake District's most valued and visited attractions.

The first room that visitors see is called the entrance hall. This is a cozy room with a stone-lagged floor and a rustic-looking fireplace. In front of the fireplace are a rocking chair and a spinning wheel. Among the many works of art displayed in the room is a small painting by the famous illustrator Randolph Caldecott, who was one of Potter's artists. Adjoining the entrance hall is the parlor. It has an elegant marble fireplace and wood-paneled walls on which hang numerous landscape paintings by such artists as Charlotte Nasmyth and John Brett. Upstairs, visitors encounter Potter's bedroom, a sitting room, her treasure room, and the room where she did her writing. These last two are perhaps the most interesting of the upstairs rooms. The tiny treasure room is filled with curios, trinkets, and miniature toys. The focal point of this room is a charming dollhouse complete with furniture. Potter's writing room, which she called the new room since it was part of the 1906 addition, is the brightest room in the house. On its walls are several large landscape paintings by her brother, Bertram Potter.

Touring the house is especially delightful for those who are familiar with Potter's picture books. At practically every turn, careful observers can spot a piece of furniture or an architectural element that Potter used in one of her books. The small covered front porch is the same one in which Mrs. Tabitha Twitchit stands while admonishing her three troublesome kittens in *The Tale of Tom Kitten* (1907). The grandfather clock located on the landing is pictured in *The Roly-Poly Pudding* (1908). The large dresser in the entrance hall also appears in *The Roly-Poly Pudding*. The miniature pieces of toy food in Potter's treasure room are the same ones that she included in *The Tale of Two Bad Mice* (1904).

As delightful as it is to see the models that Potter used for many of her illustrations, what is even more impressive is how Potter's presence still permeates the house. Perhaps because everything in the house meant something to Potter, visitors immediately sense a personality amid the furniture, paintings, and curios. Through the house and its furnishings, Potter expressed her appreciation of craftsmanship, her love of nature, and her enjoyment of the fanciful. In a sense, to visit Hill Top Farm is to visit Beatrix Potter.

Visitor Information:

Hill Top Farm is located two miles south of Hawkshead on B5285. It is open daily except on Thursday and Friday. From March to May it is open from 11:00 a.m. to 4:30 p.m. From June to August it is open from 10:30 a.m. to 5:00 p.m. In September and October, it is open from 11:00 a.m. to 4:30 p.m. Hill Top Farm is closed to the public from November through the end of February. On busy days, visitors sometimes have to wait to enter. An admission fee is charged. For more information, contact:

> Hill Top Farm
> Near Sawrey
> Ambleside, Cumbria
> LA22 0LF
> Tel: 015394 3624
> E-mail: rp.m.ht@smtp.ntrust.org.uk

The House of *The Tailor of Gloucester*

Gloucester, Gloucestershire

Beatrix Potter never lived in Gloucester, but on several occasions she went to Gloucester to visit her cousin Caroline Hutton. On one of these visits, she heard a story about a tailor who had been hired to make a waistcoat for the mayor. According to the story, the tailor had left the unfinished coat in his shop one Friday. When he returned on Monday he was surprised to see that some unseen fairies had mysteriously completed the coat. Potter liked the story and used it as the basis for her second picture book, *The Tailor of Gloucester* (1903). In her version, however, she decided to use mice instead of fairies.

Potter based her pictures of the tailor's shop on a real building located near the famous Gloucester Cathedral. While in Gloucester, she made preliminary sketches of the building and its surroundings. She later referred to these sketches when she was completing the actual illustrations for the book. Potter placed the tailor's shop on Westgate Street, and she included several pictures of this street in the finished book.

The building that Potter used as the model for the tailor's shop is now open to the public. Scattered around the building are displays about Potter's life and work as well as tableaux based on Potter's illustrations. The building also functions as a Beatrix Potter shop. It offers a vast assortment of books, toys, chinaware, and other material featuring Potter's famous characters.

Visitor Information:

The House of *The Tailor of Gloucester* is located on the corner of Westgate Street and College Court. It is open Monday through Saturday from 9:30 a.m. to 5:30 p.m. There is a small admission fee. For more information, contact:

>The House of *The Tailor of Gloucester*
>9 College Court
>Gloucester, Gloucestershire
>G11 2NJ
>Tel: 01452-422856

Melford Hall

Long Melford, Suffolk

Built between 1554 and 1578, Melford Hall is one of the most stately homes in Suffolk. The Hall is famous for its many turrets, cupolas, and tall chimneys as well as for its elaborate garden. In 1786, Sir Harry Parker purchased the Hall, and it remained in the Parker family until 1960, when it was transferred to the National Trust.

Beatrix Potter visited Melford Hall on several occasions to see her cousin Ethel, Lady Hyde Parker, who lived at the Hall. While visiting her cousin, Potter worked on the illustrations for both *The Tailor of Gloucester* (1903) and *The Tale of Squirrel Nutkin* (1903). She even asked the gamekeeper to catch her a squirrel that she could use for a model. In commemoration of Potter's association's with Melford Hall, an upstairs bedroom has been designated the Beatrix Potter Room. On display in this room are several of Potter's original watercolors depicting the Hall and the surrounding gardens. The room also includes a toy version of Jemima Puddleduck, which Potter gave to one of the children in the family.

Visitor Information:

Melford Hall is in the village of Long Melford on the eastern side of A134. From May through September, it is open on Wednesday, Thursday, Friday, Saturday, and Sunday from 2:00 p.m. to 5:30 p.m. In April and in October, it is open on Saturday and Sunday from 2:00 p.m. to 5:30 p.m. An admission fee is charged. For more information, contact:

Melford Hall
Long Melford
Sudbury, Suffolk
CO10 9AA
Tel: 01787 880286

Beatrix Potter Gallery

Hawkshead, Cumbria

Beatrix Potter's husband, William Heelis, had his law office in a seventeenth-century building located in the village of Hawkshead. After Heelis's death in August 1945, his office continued to be used as a law office. For many years, the building served as the Hawkshead branch for the law firm of Gatey, Heelis & Co. In 1987, however, this firm decided to close its Hawkshead branch, and shortly thereafter the National Trust acquired the building. With financial help from the Frederick Warne publishing company, the National Trust turned the building into a museum and gallery devoted to lives and work of Beatrix Potter and William Heelis.

During the building's renovation, part of William Heelis's law office was carefully re-created. Several pieces of the original furniture were found and put on display in the office. The National Trust also put on display numerous photographs of Heelis and Potter as well as members of their extended families.

Four rooms of the building were converted into gallery space that the National Trust then used to display its large collection of Potter's artwork. Since the opening of the Beatrix Potter Gallery, the National Trust has mounted an annually changing exhibition of Potter's original illustrations from her picture books.

Visitor Information:

The Beatrix Potter Gallery is located on Main Street in the middle of Hawkshead. From April through October, it is open on Sunday, Monday, Tuesday, Wednesday, and Thursday from 10:30 a.m. to 4:30 p.m. An admission fee is charged. For more information, contact:

Beatrix Potter Gallery
Main Street
Hawkshead, Cumbria
LA22 0NS
Tel: 015394 36355
E-mail: rhabpg@smtp.ntrust.org.uk

The Armitt Library and Museum

Ambleside, Cumbria

Founded in 1909 and opened in 1912, the Armitt Library initially collected books about the history, culture, and geography of the Lake District. Soon, however, it began adding manuscripts, original works of art, and memorabilia to its holdings. In 1933, it opened a museum room to display some of these items. The Armitt moved to a new and much larger building in 1997, and since then the museum has added new displays, including one devoted to Beatrix Potter's work.

Potter took an interest in the Armitt in the early 1930s. At the time, the Armitt was collecting materials related to the excavation of an old Roman fort near Ambleside. This development prompted Potter to give the Armitt a collection of her watercolor paintings of Roman objects. In 1943, she donated a large collection of her scientific drawings and paintings of fungi.

Today the Armitt Library and Museum maintains a permanent exhibit on Potter and her pictures of fungi. This exhibit does not include all of the Armitt's Potter holdings, but it does provide a representative sample of this aspect of Potter's work. For visitors who want to learn more about Potter's fascination with fungi, the gift shop sells a helpful booklet by Elizabeth Battrick on the topic. It's titled *Beatrix Potter: The Unknown Years*, and it's published by the Armitt Library.

Visitor Information:

The Armitt Library and Museum is located on Rydal Road in Ambleside. It is open daily from 10 a.m. to 5:00 p.m. An admission fee is charged. For more information, contact:

Armitt Library and Museum
Rydal Road
Ambleside, Cumbria
LA22 9BL
Tel: 015394 31212
E-mail: almc@armitt.com
Website: www.armitt.com

Victoria and Albert Museum

South Kensington, London

During her years in London, Beatrix Potter frequently visited the South Kensington Museum, which was renamed the Victoria and Albert Museum in 1909. She often did sketches of the pictures and objects that she saw at this famous art museum. While working on the illustrations for *The Tailor of Gloucester*, for example, she examined the museum's collection of eighteenth-century clothing and made sketches of particular articles of clothing. In several cases, the characters in the book are dressed in clothing that Potter had sketched during this visit.

After moving to the Lake District, Potter stopped making regular visits to the South Kensington Museum, but this move did not mark the end of her association with the museum. Thirty years after her death, the Victoria and Albert Museum came into possession of a large collection of Potter's drawings, manuscripts, and early editions of her books. This material was bequeathed to the museum by Leslie Linder, one of the first scholars to take an interest in the life and work of Beatrix Potter.

For the most part, the Victoria and Albert's Potter collection is open only to researchers who obtain permission to examine the material prior to visiting the museum. However, examples from the museum's Potter collection are exhibited in a display case located in the corridor next to the museum's restaurant. A new selection is put on exhibit every four months.

Visitor Information:

Located in South Kensington, the Victoria and Albert Museum is on Cromwell Road next door to the Natural History Museum. It is open daily from 10:00 a.m. to 5:45 p.m. An admission fee is charged, but children under the age of eighteen are admitted free of charge. For more information, contact:

> The Victoria and Albert Museum
> Cromwell Road
> South Kensington, London
> SW7 2RL
> Tel: 0171 938 8500
> E-mail: nal.enquiries@vam.ac.uk
> Website: www.nal.vam.ac.uk

The World of Beatrix Potter Attraction

Bowness-on-Windermere, Cumbria

Of the various Beatrix Potter sites that are open to the public, the one that children usually like the most is the World of Beatrix Potter Attraction. This site is located in the heart of Potter's beloved Lake District, but the actual site has no direct connection to Potter's life or work.

This attraction features a series of three-dimensional representations of scenes from Potter's picture books. Created by a team of artists and technicians who had previously designed sets for the National Theatre and the Royal Shakespeare Company, each diorama is true to Potter's artistic style.

In addition to examining the dioramas, visitors can view a video about Potter's life, try several interactive puzzles, and purchase Potter-related merchandise in the gift shop. The attraction also features its own Tailor of Gloucester Tearoom, where visitors can eat lunch or sip a cup of tea.

Visitor Information:

The World of Beatrix Potter Attraction is located in the middle of Bowness-on-Windermere in the building that once housed the Windermere Steam Laundry Company. The attraction is open daily. From the beginning of April to the end of September, it is open from 10:00 a.m. to 5:30 p.m. From the beginning of October to the end of March, it is open from 10:00 a.m. to 4:30 p.m. An admission fee is charged. For more information, contact:

    The World of Beatrix Potter Attraction
    The Old Laundry
    Bowness-on-Windermere, Cumbria
    LA23 3BX
    Tel: 015394 88444
    E-mail: enquiries@hop-skip-jump.com
    Website: www.hop-skip-jump.com

20
Arthur Ransome

The two children's authors most frequently associated with the Lake District are Beatrix Potter and Arthur Ransome (1884-1967). Although Potter and Ransome did not know each other, their lives had several points in common. During their youths, both spent many summer holidays in the Lake District. Both felt inspired by the Lake District's natural beauty, and both set many of their children's books in this area. Eventually, both became permanent residents of the Lake District. These two authors, however, did not write the same type of children's books. Whereas Potter created brief picture books, Ransome wrote a series of lengthy adventure stories about children who are vacationing in the Lake District.

Ransome was born and raised in Leeds, where his father taught history at the local college. His father, however, enjoyed fishing over teaching. Each summer his father took the family to the Lake District, where he rented a farm on Coniston Water. His father taught Arthur Ransome how to fish, handle a boat, and play various outdoor sports. Arthur never became as skilled an outdoorsman as his father was, but he soon came to share his father's passionate love of the Lake District.

After graduating from Rugby, Ransome briefly attended Leeds University, where he studied chemistry. He quickly realized that chemistry wasn't for him and instead set out to pursue a career as a freelance writer. At first he wrote articles about outdoor sports and various other topics. Eventually he became an overseas correspondent for the *Daily News*, *The Observer*, and the *Manchester Guardian*, filing stories from such places as Russia, Egypt, and China. He became especially well known for the pieces he wrote while living in Russia. During his time in Russia, he met Leon Trotsky's secretary, a woman named Evgenia Shelepin, and the two fell in love. After living together for several years, they were married in 1924.

Ransome wrote several books during his career as a journalist, the most important of which was *Six Weeks in Russia in 1919* (1919). He also wrote a short children's book titled *Old Peter's Russian Tales* (1917). He found that he enjoyed writing books more than filing news stories. Thus, in the late 1920s, he decided to leave journalism and try his hand at writing a substantial novel for children.

Drawing on his memories of the summer holidays of his youth, he created a story about two families who are spending the summer in the Lake District. The children in one family go sailing in a dinghy called *Swallow*, while the children in the other family sail a boat named *Amazon*. At first the children from these two families do not get along, but they soon become friends and go on many adventures together. Ransome titled the book *Swallows and Amazons*. It came out in 1930 and met with considerable success. Encouraged, he continued to write about these characters and their adventures in eleven other books, including *Peter Duck* (1932), *Winter Holiday* (1933), *We Didn't Mean to Go to Sea* (1937), and *The Picts and the Martyrs* (1943).

In 1940, Ransome made the Lake District his primary home, although he sometimes spent the winter months in London. His last book, *Mainly about Fishing*, came out in 1959 and dealt largely with his experiences as a fisherman in the Lake District. That same year he suffered a bad fall, after which his health steadily declined. He spent his final eighteen months in a hospital in Manchester. He died on June 3, 1967. In accordance with his wishes, he was buried in the Lake District. He chose as his final resting place the Rusland churchyard, a peaceful and secluded spot located about halfway between Lake Windermere and Coniston Water.

Museum of Lakeland Life

Kendal, Cumbria

The Museum of Lakeland Life focuses on the cultural history of the Lake District. Shortly after Ransome died, his widow, Evgenia, donated to the museum numerous books and other items that had belonged to her husband. The museum created an Arthur Ransome Room to display this material.

The Ransome Room resembles a study. It includes copies of all the books he wrote, some of his manuscripts and original drawings, and the Remington portable typewriter that he used. Also on display are his pipes, fishing rods, and his favorite chess set.

The museum also serves as the headquarters for the Arthur Ransome Society. Formed in 1990, this organization has about 1,300 members. It sponsors scholarly meetings, outdoor events, and other activities that relate to Ransome's life and work. Membership forms are available at the museum.

Visitor Information:

The Museum of Lakeland Life is adjacent to the Abbot Hall Art Gallery. These facilities are located at the southern end of Kendal, overlooked by Kendal Castle. The museum is open daily from 10:30 a.m. to 5:00 p.m. The museum is closed from late December until early February. An admission fee is charged. For more information, contact:

Museum of Lakeland Life
Abbot Hall
Kendal, Cumbria
LA9 5Al
Tel: 01539 722464
E-mail: ws@lakelandmuseum.org.uk
Website: www.lakelandmuseum.org.uk

Windermere Steamboat Centre

Windermere, Cumbria

Opened in 1977, the Windermere Steamboat Centre has a large collection of steam yachts and other boats that once plied Lake Windermere or some of the other bodies of water in the Lake District. Of the boats on display, two have connections to Ransome's *Swallows and Amazons*.

At one point in *Swallows and Amazons*, the children spot a houseboat owned by a character named Captain Flint. The boat is described as "a long narrow craft with a high raised roof, and a row of glass windows along her side. Her bows were like the bows of an old-time clipper. Her stern was like that of a steamship." This boat and its eccentric owner figure very prominently in the second half of the book. Ransome based this boat a real steam yacht named *Esperance*, which was built in 1869. The *Esperance* sank in 1941, but it was successfully salvaged, and it is now one of the Steamboat Centre's chief attractions.

The center also has on display a small sailboat that Ransome probably used as the inspiration for the *Amazon*. The boat was originally called *Mavis*, but after its restoration in 1989, it was renamed *Amazon*.

Visitor Information:

The Windermere Steamboat Centre is located on Rayrigg Road in Windermere. The center is open daily from 10:00 a.m. to 5:00 p.m. It is closed from the beginning of November to the middle of March. An admission fee is charged. For more information, contact:

Windermere Steamboat Centre
Rayrigg Road
Windermere, Cumbria
LA23 1BN
Tel: 015394 45565
Website: www.steamboat.co.uk

21
Robin Hood

The legend of Robin Hood, like the legend of King Arthur, has a long and murky history. Some scholars argue that the legend is based on a real person who lived in the twelfth century, while others argue that the legend is tied to an early mythological figure. Robin Hood made his debut in English literature in 1377, when William Langland mentioned the name in his famous poem "Piers Plowman." During the 1400s and 1500s, balladeers often sang of Robin Hood's exploits, and the verses they sang served as the basis for later prose versions of the legend.

In 1795, Joseph Ritson collected a number of Robin Hood ballads and published them in a book titled *Robin Hood Garlands*. Ritson's collection not only stirred interest in the Robin Hood legend, but also served as a sort of sourcebook for several nineteenth-century novelists. Thomas Hood, for example, drew on Ritson's research when writing his novel *Maid Marian* (1822). Riston's book also inspired Sir Walter Scott, who included both Robin Hood and Friar Tuck in his novel *Ivanhoe* (1819).

The history of Robin Hood's associations with children's literature can be traced to the publication of Pierce Egan's *Robin Hood and Little John* in 1840. Since then, numerous children's books about Robin Hood have appeared, including Howard Pyle's *The Merry Adventures of Robin Hood* (1893), Geoffrey Trease's *Bows against the Barons* (1934), Rosemary Sutcliff's *The Chronicles of Robin Hood* (1950), Roger Lancelyn Green's *The Adventures of Robin Hood* (1956), and Jane Louise Curry's *Robin Hood and His Merry Men* (1994).

Sherwood Forest Country Park & Visitor Centre

Edwinstowe, Nottinghamshire

Robin Hood may or may not have been a real person, but there is no denying that Sherwood Forest, Robin Hood's famous haunt, is a real place. Since the end of the last Ice Age, the site of today's Sherwood Forest has been a woodland area. In the Middle Ages, Sherwood Forest was designated a royal hunting preserve, which meant that anyone who cut timber or hunted in the forest without the king's permission faced severe punishments. In those days, the forest covered more than 100,000 acres. Today Sherwood Forest has been reduced to approximately 450 acres, but the forest that remains looks much as it did during the Middle Ages.

Made up primarily of birch and oak trees, Sherwood Forest is home to more than 900 trees that are at least 600 years old. The most famous tree in the forest is the Major Oak. According to the legend, Robin Hood often hid in the hollow center of this tree. It is easy to see why this tree has come to be associated with the Robin Hood legend, for it is the sort of tree that sparks the imagination. Horticultural experts estimate that the Major Oak is more than 800 years old. The statistics related to its size are also impressive. Its girth is thirty-three feet, and the spread of its branches measures ninety-two feet.

Sherwood Forest is now a country park with an official visitor center, nature trails, and a restaurant. There are several places in the park that are of particular interest to visitors who are intrigued with the forest's associations with the Robin Hood legend. Located just outside the Visitor Centre is a large statue of Robin Hood and Little John tussling on a wooden bridge. Visitors can also tour "Robyn Hode's Sherwode Exhibition," which combines material about the legend of Robin Hood with factual information about the forest.

The park has two on-site shops, where visitors can buy books about Robin Hood, all sorts of Robin Hood memorabilia, toy archery sets, and even Robin Hood costumes. Lots of children manage to talk their parents into buying these costumes, which is why you can still find green-clad free spirits romping through Sherwood Forest in search of the Major Oak.

Visitor Information:

Sherwood Forest Country Park & Visitor Centre is situated on the B6034 just north of the village of Edwinstowe. The park is open daily from dawn to dusk. The Visitor Centre opens at 10:30 a.m. and closes at 5:00 p.m. From November through March, the Visitor Centre closes at 4:30 p.m. Admission is free, but a small parking fee is charged from April to October. For more information, contact:

> Sherwood Forest Country Park & Visitor Centre
> Edwinstowe
> Mansfield
> Nottinghamshire
> NG21 9HN
> Tel: 01623/823202

The Tales of Robin Hood Visitor Attraction

Nottingham, Nottinghamshire

After Sherwood Forest, the place most frequently associated with Robin Hood is Nottingham. Everyone who has heard of Robin Hood knows about his antagonistic relationship with the Sheriff of Nottingham. Those who are familiar with the details of the legend know that Robin Hood often disguised himself and visited Nottingham to gain information, rescue a friend, or play a trick on the sheriff.

In Robin Hood's time, the town officials didn't exactly welcome Robin Hood, but nowadays Nottingham celebrates its association with the legend of Robin Hood. There is a large statue of Robin Hood near Nottingham Castle, one of the main streets is called Maid Marian Way, and many businesses are named after characters from the legend. Still, for many years Nottingham lacked a central tourist attraction that focused on Robin Hood. In the late 1980s, the Nottingham City Council responded to this problem by creating the Tales of Robin Hood Visitor Attraction. This facility opened in 1989, and has since become one of Nottingham's most popular tourist destinations.

Located on Maid Marian Way, the Tales of Robin Hood Visitor Attraction provides today's tourists with an opportunity to travel back in time to the age of Robin Hood. Visitors board small "adventure cars," which take them through an elaborate re-creation of the sights, sounds, and smells of medieval Nottingham. After disembarking from the ride, visitors can try their hand at archery, watch a short film about Robin Hood, view a falconry display, and buy Robin Hood memorabilia in the gift shop.

Visitor Information:

The Tales of Robin Hood Visitor Attraction is situated in Nottingham City Centre, just a two-minute walk from Nottingham Castle. Its address is 30-38 Maid Marian Way. The attraction is open daily from 10:00 a.m. to 6:00 p.m. Last admission for the ride is 4:30 p.m. An admission fee is charged. For more information, contact:

The Tales of Robin Hood Visitor Attraction
30-38 Maid Marian Way
Nottingham, Nottinghamshire
NG1 6GF
Tel: 0115 9483284
E-mail: support@robinhood.uk.com
Website: www.robinhood.uk.com

22
Robert Louis Stevenson

Robert Louis Stevenson (1850-1894) spent his childhood and early adult years in Edinburgh. The only child of a wealthy engineer, Stevenson was expected to follow in his father's footsteps, but Stevenson knew from an early age that he did not want to be an engineer. After halfheartedly studying the law at Edinburgh University, he left Scotland and began his writing career. He lived in many places during his brief life, including Monterey, California; Davos, Switzerland; St. Marcel, France; Bournemouth, England; Saranac Lake, New York; and finally Upolu, a large island in Western Samoa. No matter where he lived, however, Stevenson thought of himself as Scottish author.

Stevenson wrote a wide variety of works, but he is best remembered for his classic children's books. Stevenson's interest in writing for children grew out of his marriage to Fanny Osbourne in 1880. She had a son named Lloyd from a previous marriage and Stevenson often told stories to his young stepson. In the summer of 1881, Lloyd and Stevenson made up a treasure map and this prompted Stevenson to write a story to go with the map. The result was *Treasure Island* (1883). Although Stevenson initially saw it as one of his less important works, the reading public embraced the book. The book was such a commercial and critical success that Stevenson felt encouraged to write additional books for children. These books include *A Child's Garden of Verses* (1885), *Kidnapped* (1886), and *The Black Arrow* (1888).

Of his children's books, *Kidnapped* has the strongest ties to Stevenson's native Scotland. Stevenson described it as an adventure story for boys, but the work is as much a book about Scotland as it is a tale of derring-do. Stevenson filled the book with so many vivid details about Scottish history, culture, and geography that it is hard to believe that he had been living away from Scotland for a number of years when he wrote it. The wealth of detail that he put into *Kidnapped* reflects the deep effect his boyhood home had on his life and writings.

Writers' Museum

Edinburgh, Scotland

During his childhood, Stevenson lived in a wealthy section of Edinburgh called New Town. He grew up in a stately home located on 17 Heriot Row, and he seldom saw the less prosperous sections of Edinburgh. While attending Edinburgh University, however, he became fascinated with the section of Edinburgh known as Old Town, which at that time was considered one of the worst slums in Great Britain.

Stevenson spent countless hours wandering through Old Town's narrow streets, frequenting its many pubs and taking advantage of the diversions that were so readily available in Old Town. His parents were appalled at their son's plunge into decadence, but Stevenson was doing more than simply pursuing hedonistic pleasures during this period in his life. He was learning about the lives of Edinburgh's poor people, from whom he had been sheltered as a child. This new knowledge caused him to reject the snobbery of New Town, and in so doing he removed the blinders that prevented some wealthy Scots from seeing the less pleasant aspects of their society. He may not have remembered much of what he learned in his classes at the university, but the lessons he learned in Old Town served him well when he became a writer.

Given the importance that Old Town played in Stevenson's life, it is fitting that Old Town is where visitors can find a major exhibit on Stevenson. This exhibit is located in the Writers' Museum, which is just a short walk from the famous Edinburgh Castle. The museum is in a tall, narrow building that dates back to the 1620s. Once a house owned by the dowager countess of Stair, it now contains exhibits on Stevenson, Robert Burns, and Walter Scott.

The Stevenson exhibit provides useful information on his family background, his writing career, and his travels. Perhaps the most interesting items on display are those that relate to Stevenson's youth. Several examples of his childhood writings can be seen. The exhibit also includes a miniature printing press that he owned as a child. Although it looks like a toy, Stevenson actually used it to print some of his first literary efforts.

Visitor Information:

The Writers' Museum is located on Lady Stair's Close, just off the Lawnmarket in Old Town. It is open from 10:00 a.m. to 5:00 p.m., Monday through Saturday. There is no admission charge. For more information, contact:

> The Writers' Museum
> Lady Stair's House
> Lady Stair's Close
> Lawnmarket
> Edinburgh, Scotland
> EH1 2PA
> Tel: 0131 529 4901

Hawes Inn

South Queensferry, Scotland

When Stevenson was twenty-one years old, he finally decided to tell his father that he wanted to become a writer rather than an engineer. Although disappointed, his father agreed to support Stevenson's new career goal. From then on, Stevenson looked at the world in a somewhat different way. He had always been an observant person, but now he began to make a conscious effort to remember details about his environment so that he could use them in his writing. If he saw something particularly interesting, he now thought about how it could figure in a story.

During this early stage in his writing career, Stevenson enjoyed taking walks to the village of South Queensferry. Located about ten miles west of Edinburgh, this village was where people went to board the ferry that crossed the Firth of Forth. He often stopped at Hawes Inn, a historic building situated a short distance from the village. Intrigued by this building, Stevenson soon began thinking about how he could work it into a story. In an essay written a few years later, he discussed his reactions to the building:

> The old Hawes Inn at the Queen's Ferry makes a call upon my fancy. There it stands, apart from the town beside the pier, in a climate of its own, half inland, half marine—in front, the ferry bubbling with the tide and the guardship swinging to her anchor; behind, the old garden with the trees. There is some story, unrecorded or not yet complete, which must express the meaning of that inn more fully.

In his memory, Stevenson filed away his impressions of Hawes Inn. He felt sure he would one day include the inn in one of his stories, but it was not until he began writing *Kidnapped* that he actually did. As readers of *Kidnapped* surely remember, Hawes Inn figures prominently in the book. David Balfour, the central character in the story, and his wicked uncle stay at Hawes Inn. While he is at the inn, David is abducted and taken aboard a ship.

Hawes Inn is still standing and open for business. The building has been expanded over the years, but the oldest part dates from the late seventeenth century. The current management of the inn celebrates the inn's connections to Stevenson in several ways. The walls of the bar are covered with Stevenson memorabilia, and the inn's restaurant, which serves a wide variety of Scottish foods, is named after Stevenson. Guest room number 13 is also named after Stevenson. This is the room where Stevenson stayed when he visited the inn while writing *Kidnapped*.

Visitor Information:

Hawes Inn is located in South Queensferry at the base of the famous Cantilever Forth Railway Bridge, which crosses the Firth of Forth. The inn features guestrooms, a bar, and its own Stevenson Restaurant. For more information, contact:

Hawes Inn
7 Newhalls Road
South Queensferry, Scotland
EH30 9TA
Tel: 0131 331 1990

23
J. R. R. Tolkien

John Roland Reuel Tolkien (1892-1973) grew up in an environment that supported the development of his fertile imagination. He was born in South Africa, but at the age of three he moved to England. His father died shortly thereafter, but his mother was able to provide Tolkien and his brother with a secure home in the village of Sarehole near Birmingham. From an early age, Tolkien took a strong liking to fairy tales and other works of fantasy, and his mother encouraged this by providing him with copies of Andrew Lang's famous collections of fairy tales. As he grew older, she gave him books about dragons and copies of George MacDonald's books, which he read avidly.

Tolkien remained interested in fantasy literature during his student years at King Edward's School, St. Philip's School, and finally Exeter College, one of the colleges that make up Oxford University. While at Oxford, he studied Old Norse, Anglo-Saxon, and several other old languages. In addition to learning these languages, he developed an expertise in the myths and folklore associated with these languages. Tolkien's knowledge of Anglo-Saxon eventually led to his being awarded a teaching position at Oxford University.

Tolkien married Edith Bratt in 1916, and they had four children between 1917 and 1929. He often made up fantasy stories for his children, and their enthusiastic response to his stories encouraged him to try his hand at writing a book for children. Around 1930 he began working on *The Hobbit*, a full-length fantasy novel for children. It took him several years to finish the book, but when it came out in 1937 it met with great success. He then went on to write his famous trilogy, which is collectively titled *The Lord of the Rings* (1954-1955). Although *The Lord of the Rings* had direct connections to *The Hobbit*, Tolkien intended his trilogy for adult readers.

The Eagle and Child

Oxford, Oxfordshire

When Tolkien was not teaching at Oxford or with his family, he enjoyed spending time with his friends at several local pubs. The two people who joined him most often were C. S. Lewis (see chapter 15) and Charles Williams, a poet, novelist, and writer of theological works. The three of them took to calling themselves the Inklings. Their favorite pub was the Eagle and Child, which they often called the Bird and Baby. This pub first opened as an inn around 1650, making it one of Oxford's oldest pubs.

From the 1930s until the early 1960s, the Inklings met at this pub nearly every week. They often read aloud passages from their works in progress. In fact, it was at the Eagle and Child that Tolkien read aloud the initial drafts of *The Hobbit*. The Inklings often critiqued each other's works after listening to these readings, and Tolkien generally appreciated this feedback.

Tolkien's love of pubs is also reflected in his writings. Although pubs do not figure in *The Hobbit*, a pub called The Prancing Pony figures prominently in *The Lord of the Rings*. This pub is where Frodo, the central character, meets Aragorn. Their meeting proves to be a pivotal point in the trilogy, for Aragorn immediately joins Frodo on his quest and soon assumes a leadership role.

Although the Eagle and Child has changed ownership several times since the days when it was frequented by Tolkien, the pub still celebrates its associations with the Inklings. The pub is divided into several alcoves. The paneled alcove where the Inklings often met has photographs of Tolkien, Lewis, and Williams displayed on the walls.

Visitor Information:

The Eagle and Child is in the central section of Oxford. It is located on the western side of St. Giles, just before the street splits and becomes

Woodstock Road. The pub is open daily. From Monday through Saturday, it is open from 11:30 a.m. to 11:00 p.m. On Sunday it opens at noon and closes at 10:30 p.m. Children are not admitted during evening hours. For more information, contact:

The Eagle and Child
49 Saint Giles
Oxford, Oxfordshire
OX1 3LU
Tel: 01865 302925

24
Mary Tourtel

Before Paddington Bear and Winnie-the-Pooh made their debuts, a bear named Rupert had already captured the imaginations of British children. Created by Mary Tourtel (1874-1948), Rupert Bear first appeared in a comic strip published by the *Daily Express* on November 8, 1920. The strip became so popular that Tourtel quickly gathered together a number of the strips and arranged to have them published in a book titled *The Adventures of Rupert, The Little Lost Bear* (1921). Soon other Rupert books appeared, including *Rupert Little Bear's Adventures* (1924), *Rupert and the Old Miser* (1925), and *The Monster Rupert* (1932).

Tourtel, whose maiden name was Caldwell, grew up in Canterbury. Her childhood ambition was to become an artist, and her father, who created and restored stained-glass windows for a living, encouraged her to develop her artistic abilities. She studied at the Sidney Cooper School of Art in Canterbury, where she won recognition for her paintings of animals. From 1897 to 1900, she studied at the Royal College of Art. During this period, she began doing illustrations for books. One of the books she illustrated was a collection of poems by Herbert Tourtel. While working together on this book, the two fell in love. They married in September 1900. Herbert Tourtel eventually became an editor for the *Daily Express*, and he was the one who suggested that his wife do a comic strip for the paper.

Mary Tourtel continued to write and illustrate Rupert Bear stories until 1935, when her failing eyesight made it too difficult for her to do the drawings. For most of her adult life, she had lived away from Canterbury, but after her retirement she returned to Canterbury. She died on March 15, 1948. Her ashes were buried in St. Martin's churchyard in Canterbury.

Canterbury Heritage Museum

Canterbury, Kent

The city of Canterbury has long taken pride in its association with Mary Tourtel. When she was an art student, the mayor of Canterbury personally presented her with a prize for her artwork. When Rupert Bear became a national celebrity, Canterbury soon claimed the bear as well as its creator. Canterbury's love affair with Rupert Bear can be seen at the Canterbury Heritage Museum.

In 1988, the Canterbury Heritage Museum mounted a special exhibit on Rupert Bear. The exhibit attracted so many visitors that it broke attendance records. The headline in the local paper proclaimed, "City in Grip of Rupert Mania." The success of this exhibit led the museum to create a permanent Rupert Bear Gallery, which opened to the public in 1992. The museum's exhibits are arranged chronologically, beginning with the Romans and ending with Rupert. It is not uncommon to see children racing through the museum in order to reach the Rupert Gallery as soon as possible.

The Rupert Bear Gallery includes material related to Mary Tourtel, including many of her original drawings of Rupert. The exhibit also features original illustrations by the other artists who continued the Rupert comic strip after Tourtel retired. These other illustrators include Alfred Bestall, who drew the strip from 1935 through 1965, and Alex Cubie, who contributed to the strip from 1965 through 1977. In addition to original artwork, the gallery has on display several large models of Rupert and some of the other animal characters that appear in the Rupert stories.

Visitor Information:

The Canterbury Heritage Museum is located on Stour Street in a historic building that was once the Poor Priests' Hospital. It is open Monday through Saturday from 10:30 a.m. to 5:00 p.m. From June through the end of October, it is also open on Sunday from 1:30 p.m. to 5:00 p.m. An admission fee is charged. For more information, contact:

Canterbury Heritage Museum
Stour Street
Canterbury, Kent
CT1 2NR
Tel: 01227 452747
Website: www.canterbury.gov.uk

Selected Bibliography

Ashe, Geoffrey. *Quest for Author's Britain.* London: Paladin, 1977.
Bates, Colleen Dunn, and Susan Latempa. *Storybook Travels.* New York: Three Rivers Press, 2002.
Battrick, Elizabeth. *Beatrix Potter: The Unknown Years.* Ambleside: Armitt Library and Museum, 1999.
Bodger, Joan. *How the Heather Looks: A Joyous Journey to the British Sources of Children's Books.* New York: Viking Press, 1965.
Brogan, Hugh. *The Life of Arthur Ransome.* London: Pimlico Press, 1984.
Carpenter, Humphrey. *The Inklings.* London: George Allen & Unwin, 1978.
Carpenter, Humphrey, and Mari Prichard. *The Oxford Companion to Children's Literature.* Oxford: Oxford University Press, 1984.
Clark, Keith. *Beatrix Potter's Gloucester.* London: Frederick Warne, 1988.
Clinch, Rosemary, and Michael Williams. *King Arthur in Somerset.* Bodmin, U.K.: Bossiney Books, 1987.
Cunningham, Ian. *A Reader's Guide to Writers' London.* London: Prion Books, 2001.
Denyer, Susan. *Beatrix Potter at Home in the Lake District.* London: Frances Lincoln Ltd., 2000.
Eagle, Dorothy, and Hilary Carnell, eds. *The Oxford Illustrated Literary Guide to Great Britain and Ireland.* 2d ed. Oxford: Oxford University Press, 1992.
Franco, L. N. *Literary Landscapes: Walking Tours in Great Britain and Ireland.* New York: George Braziller Publisher, 1998.
Green, Peter. *Beyond the Wild Wood: The World of Kenneth Grahame.* Exeter: Webb & Bower, 1982.

Helbig, Alethea K., and Agnes Regan Perkins. *Dictionary of British Children's Fiction*. Westport, Conn.: Greenwood Press, 1989.
Holt, J.C. *Robin Hood*. London: Thames & Hudson, 1984.
Hunt, Peter. *Approaching Arthur Ransome*. London: Jonathan Cape, 1984.
Kendall-Price, Claire. *In the Footsteps of the Swallows and Amazons*. York, U.K.: Wildcat Publishing, 1993.
Matthewa, John. *Robin Hood: Green Lord of the Wildwood*. Glastonbury: Gothic Image Publications, 1993.
Milne, Christopher. *The Enchanted Places*. London: Eyre Methuen, 1974.
Ousby, Ian. *Blue Guide to Literary Britain and Ireland*. 2d ed. London: A.& C. Black, 1990.
Stewart, Brian. *The Rupert Bear Dossier*. London: Hawk Books, 1997.
Tagholm, Roger. *Walking Literary London*. Chicago: Passport Books, 2001.
Taylor, Judy. *Beatrix Potter and Hawkshead*. London: National Trust, 1988.
———. *Beatrix Potter and Hill Top*. London: National Trust, 1989.
Varlow, Sally. *A Reader's Guide to Writers' Britain*. London: Prion Books, 1997.
Wardale, Roger. *In Search of Swallows & Amazons: Arthur Ransome's Lakeland*. Wilmslow, U.K.: Sigma Leisure, 1996.
West, Mark I. *Wellsprings of Imagination: The Homes of Children's Authors*. New York: Neal-Schuman, 1992.

Index

The Adventures of Robin Hood (Green), 109
The Adventures of Rupert (Tourtel), 121
Alice in Wonderland Centre, 32-33
Alice's Adventures in Wonderland (Carroll), 27-33
Alice's Adventures Underground (Carroll), 28
Alice's Shop, 30-31
Armitt Library and Museum, 100-101
Arthur, King, 3-10
Arthurian Centre, 7-8
Ashdown Forest, 82-83
Auld Licht Idylls (Barrie), 15
Awdry, Christopher, 11-13
Awdry, Wilbert, 11-13

Barrie, James M., 15-18
Barrie's Birthplace, 16-17
Bassett-Lowke, Waynne, 12
Bateman's, 65-67
Battrick, Elizabeth, 101
A Bear Called Paddington (Bond), 19-20
Beatrix Potter Gallery, 99-100
Beatrix Potter: The Unknown Years (Battrick), 101
The BFG (Dahl), 39

Black Arrow (Stevenson), 113
Blake, Quentin, 40
Bland, Hubert, 85
Blyton, Enid, 44
Bond, Michael, 19-21
The Book of King Arthur and His Noble Knights (MacLeod), 4
A Book of Nonsense (Lear), 70
Boston, Lucy, 1
Bows against the Barons (Trease), 109
The Boys' King Arthur (Lanier), 4
Broccoli, Albert, 43
Buckinghamshire County Museum, 40-41
Burnett, Frances Hodgson, 23-25
Burwash, 65-67

Cadbury Castle, 5-7
Caldecott, Randolph, 93, 96
Cambridge University, 60, 75
Cammaerts, Emile, 70
Canterbury, 121-23
Canturbury Heritage Museum, 122-23
Captains Courageous (Kipling), 63
Carnegie Medal, 76, 89
Carroll, Lewis, 27-33
Cars of the Stars Motor Museum, 44-45

Charlie and the Chocolate Factory (Dahl), 39
The Children of Green Knowe (Boston), 1
A Child's Garden of Verses (Stevenson), 113
Chitty-Chitty-Bang-Bang (Fleming), 43-45
Christ Church College, 27, 29-30
Chronicles of Narnia (Lewis), 75-77
The Chronicles of Robin Hood (Sutcliff), 109
Clovelly Visitor Centre, 60-61
Coniston Water, 105-106
Crosland, Felicity, 40
Crystal Palace Park, 86-88
Cunliffe, John, 35-37
Curry, Jane Louise, 109

Dahl, Roald, 39-41
The Dinosaurs of Waterhouse Hawkins (Kerley), 87
Dodgson, Charles Lutwidge. *See* Carroll, Lewis
Dream Days (Grahame), 48

The Eagle and Child, 76, 118-119
Edinburgh, 113-15
Edward Lear Hotel, 73-74
Egan, Pierce, 109
Ely Cathedral, 90-91
The Enchanted Castle (Nesbit), 86-87
The Enchanted Places (Milne), 82, 84

Fantastic Mr. Fox (Dahl), 39-40
Farmer Barnes Buys a Pig (Cunliffe), 35
Five Children and It (Nesbit), 86
Fleming, Ian, 43-45
Fortnum, Peggy, 19-20
Fraser, George MacDonald, 54
Frith, Henry, 4

Glasscock, Frederick Thomas, 9-10
Glastonbury Abbey, 8-9
Glastonbury Tor, 6
Glaucus; or, The Wonders of the Shore (Kingsley), 59
Gleanings from the Menagerie and Aviary at Knowsley Hall (Lear), 70
Gloucester, 97-98
Gogarth Abbey Hotel, 32
The Golden Age (Grahame), 48
Grahame, Alastair, 48-49
Grahame, Kenneth, viii, 47-52, 80
Great Maytham Hall, 24-25
Green, Roger Lancelyn, 4, 76, 109
Guildford Museum, 31-32

Hartfield, 84
Hatherell, William, 10
Hawes Inn, 115-16
Hawkins, Benjamin Waterhouse, 86-87
Hawkshead, 99-100
Heelis, William, 95
The Heroes (Kingsley), 59
Hill Top Farm, 95-97
The Hobbit (Tolkien), 117-18
Holy Trinity Church, 76-77
The Horse and His Boy (Lewis), 76
The House at Pooh Corner (Milne), 79, 82
Hughes, Thomas, 53-57
The Hunting of the Snark (Carroll), 28
Hutton, Caroline, 97

Illustrated Excursions in Italy (Lear), 70
Itinerary (Leland), 6
It's Too Late Now (Milne), 80
Ivanhoe (Scott), 109

James and the Giant Peach (Dahl), 39-40

Jock the New Engine (Awdry), 12
Journal of a Landscape Painter in Calabria (Lear), 74
The Jungle Book (Kipling), 63-64, 66
Just So Stories for Little Children (Kipling), 63

Kensington Gardens, 15, 18
Kerley, Barbara, 87
Kidnapped (Stevenson), 113-16
Kim (Kipling), 63
King Arthur and His Knights (Pyle), 4
King Arthur and His Knights of the Round Table (Frith), 4
King Arthur and the Knights of the Round Table (Green), 4
King Arthur's Great Halls, 9-10
Kingsley, Charles, 59-61
Kipling, Rudyard, 63-67
Kirriemuir, 15-17
Knowles, James T., 3
Knowsley Hall, 69-70
Knowsley Safari Park, 72-73

Lake District, 35-37, 44, 94-97, 105-108
Lang, Andrew, 117
Lanier, Sidney, 4
The Last Battle (Lewis), 76
Laughable Lyrics (Lear), 70
Lear, Edward, 69-74
Leland, John, 6
Lewis, Clive Staples, 75-77, 118
Lewis, Warren, 75, 77
Liddell, Alice, 28, 30, 32
Liddell, Henry George, 28
Linder, Leslie, 102
The Lion, the Witch, and the Wardrobe (Lewis), 75
Little Lord Fauntleroy (Burnett), 23-24
A Little Princess (Burnett), 24
The Little White Bird (Barrie), 16
Llandudno, 32-33

London Zoo, 69-72, 80-81
The Lord of the Rings (Tolkien), 118
Lycett, Andrew, 43

MacDonald, George, 75
MacLeod, Mary, 4
Madam How and Lady Why (Kingsley), 59
The Magic City (Nesbit), 86-87
The Magician's Nephew (Lewis), 76
Maid Marian (Hood), 109
Mainly about Fishing (Ransome), 106
Mapledurham House, 49-51
Matilda (Dahl), 39-40
Melford Hall, 98-99
Merlin's Cave, 4
The Merry Adventures of Robin Hood (Pyle), 109
Milne, Alan Alexander, 79-84
Milne, Christopher, 79-84
The Monster Rupert (Tourtel), 121
More about Paddington (Bond), 19
More Nonsense (Lear), 70
Museum of Lakeland Life, 36-37, 106-107

Neal, Patricia, 39
Nelson, Peter D., 44
Nesbit, Edith, 85-88
Nobel Prize, 66
Nonsense Songs, Stories, Botany, and Alphabets (Lear), 70
Nottingham, 111-12
Now We Are Six (Milne), 80

Old Peter's Russian Tales (Ransome), 106
Out of the Silent Planet (Lewis), 75
Oxford, 29-31, 75-77
Oxford University, 27, 47, 54, 75, 117

Paddington Abroad (Bond), 19
Paddington Helps Out (Bond), 19
Paddington Station, viii, 20-21
Pagan Papers (Grahame), 48
Pearce, Philippa, 89-91
Peter and Wendy (Barrie), 16
Peter Duck (Ransome), 106
Peter Pan and Wendy (Barrie), 15-16
Peter Pan Statue, 18
The Phoenix and the Carpet (Nesbit), 86
The Picts and the Martyrs (Ransome), 106
The Pilgrim's Regress (Lewis), 75
The Poetry of Nonsense (Cammaerts), 70
Pooh Corner, 84
Postman Pat and the Treasure Hunt (Cunliffe), 35
Potter, Beatrix, viii, 35, 93-103
Prince Caspian (Lewis), 76
Puck of Pook's Hill (Kipling), 63, 66
Punch, 79
Pyle, Howard, 4, 109

Ransome, Arthur, 35, 105-108
Ratcliffe, Muriel, 32
Ratcliffe, Murry, 32
Ravenglass & Eskdale Railway, 12-13
Regent's Park, 71-72, 80-81
Rewards and Fairies (Kipling), 63, 66
Ritson, Joseph, 109
Roald Dahl Children's Gallery, 40-41
Robin Hood, 109-112
Robin Hood and His Merry Men (Curry), 109
Robin Hood and Little John (Egan), 109
Robin Hood Garlands (Ritson), 109

The Roly-Poly Pudding (Potter), 96
Rottingdean, 64-65
Rowling, J. K., 54
Rugby School, 53, 56-57, 105
Rugby School Museum, 56-57
Rupert and the Old Miser (Tourtel), 121
Rupert Little Bear's Adventures (Tourtel), 121

Sara Crewe (Burnett), 23
Scott, Walter, 109
The Scouring of the White Horse (Hughes), 54
The Screwtape Letters (Lewis), 75
The Second Jungle Book (Kipling), 63, 66
The Secret Garden (Burnett), 24-25
Selznick, Brian, 87
Shepard, Ernest H., 48, 50, 52, 82
Sherwood Forest, 2, 110-111
Sherwood Forest Country Park & Visitor Centre, 110-111
The Silver Chair (Lewis), 76
Six Weeks in Russia (Ransome), 106
Slaughterbridge Stone, 7
Small Railway Engines (Awdry), 12-13
Something of Myself (Kipling), 64
Stalky & Co. (Kipling), 63
Stevenson, Robert Lewis, 113-116
The Story of King Arthur (Knowles), 3
The Story of the Amulet (Nesbit), 86
The Story of the Treasure Seekers (Nesbit), 85
Sutcliff, Rosemary, 109
Swallows and Amazons (Ransome), 106-108
The Sword in the Stone (White), 4
Sylvie and Bruno (Carroll), 28

Index

Sylvie and Bruno Concluded (Carroll), 28

The Tailor of Gloucester (Potter), 97-98
The Tale of Peter Rabbit (Potter), 93-95
The Tale of Squirrel Nutkin (Potter), 98
The Tale of Tom Kitten (Potter), 96
The Tale of Two Bad Mice (Potter), 96
Tales of Robin Hood Visitor Attraction, 111-12
Tenniel, John, 28, 30
Thames River, 47-51
Thames Rivercruise, 49-50
Thomas the Tank Engine (Awdry), 11
The Three Railway Engines (Awdry), 11
Through the Looking-Glass and What Alice Found There (Carroll), 27-28, 30
Tintagel Castle, 4-5
Toad of Toad Hall (Milne), 80
Tolkien, John Roland Reuel, 76, 117-19
Tom Brown at Oxford (Hughes), 54
Tom Brown's School Museum, 55-56
Tom Brown's Schooldays (Hughes), 53-55
Tom's Midnight Garden (Pearce), 89-91

Tourtel, Mary, 121-23
Trease, Geoffrey, 109
Treasure Island (Stevenson), 113

Uffington, 53, 55

Victoria and Albert Museum, 101-102
Voyage of the Dawn Treader (Lewis), 76

Ward, Edmund, 11
The Water-Babies (Kingsley), 59-60
We Didn't Mean to Go to Sea (Ransome), 106
Westward Ho! (Kingsley), 59
Wet Magic (Nesbit), 86
Whall, Veronica, 10
When We Were Very Young (Milne), 80-81
White, T. H., 4
Williams, Charles, 118
The Wind in the Willows (Grahame), viii, 47-52, 80
Wind in the Willows Attraction, 51-52
Windermere Steamboat Centre, 107-108
A Window in Thrums (Barrie), 15
Winnie-the-Pooh (Milne), vii, 79-84
Winter Holiday (Ransome), 106
The Witches (Dahl), 39
The World of Beatrix Potter Attraction, 102-103
Writers' Museum, 114-15

About the Author

Mark I. West is a professor of English at the University of North Carolina at Charlotte, where he teaches courses on children's literature and serves as the associate dean for general education. He has written or edited numerous books that deal with various aspects of children's literature, including *Children, Culture, and Controversy* (1988), *Trust Your Children: Voices against Censorship in Children's Literature* (1988, 2nd ed. 1997), *Roald Dahl* (1992), *Wellsprings of Imagination: The Homes of Children's Authors* (1992), *Everyone's Guide to Children's Literature* (1997), and *Psychoanalytic Responses to Children's Literature* coauthored with Lucy Rollin (1999). He is also the editor of *The Five Owls* and the book review editor of the *Children's Literature Association Quarterly*.